Homer's Porch

Homer's Porch

A Tribute to a Father

Homer Myers

WinePressPublishing
Great Books, Defined.

WinePress Publishing (PO Box 428, Enumclaw, WA 98022) functions only as book publisher. As such, the ultimate design, content, editorial accuracy, and views expressed or implied in this work are those of the author.

Unless otherwise noted, all Scriptures are taken from the *New American Standard Bible*, © 1960, 1963, 1968, 1971, 1972, 1973, 1975, 1977 by The Lockman Foundation. Used by permission.

Scripture references marked THE MESSAGE are taken from *The Message Bible* © 1993 by Eugene N. Peterson, NavPress, PO Box 35001, Colorado Springs, CO 80935, 4th printing in USA 1994. Published in association with the literary agency—Alive Comm. PO Box 49068, Colorado Springs, CO 80949. Used by permission.

ISBN 13: 978-1-4141-1850-5
ISBN 10: 1-4141-1850-3
Library of Congress Catalog Card Number: 2010908412

*In memory of my father: a teacher, coach,
principal, school superintendent,
father, husband, and great storyteller.*

Contents

Foreword

I first met Homer Lockwood Myers in the spring of 1965 when we competed on opposing track teams during our freshman year of high school. Amiable and soft-spoken, just like his kinfolk, we easily became friends when we realized that we lived just a few miles apart. Enhancing our relationship further was Homer Lockwood's transfer to old South Hall High School, where we made many memories together with our teammates on the gridiron and around the old cinder and clay track that encircled the field. While his family called him by his middle name, "Lockwood," I usually called him "Lock," and his teachers and classmates referenced him as "Homer."

BETWEEN THE TWO of us, we usually managed to have at least one vehicle in running condition during football season, but by track season our prospects often narrowed to relying on the "ankle express" for the three-and-one-half miles to my house or another couple of miles farther to his. This made it convenient for me to abandon my own family when an ice storm would disrupt our power. As they toasted bread in the fireplace, I would slip off to Lock's house where his momma would have a full breakfast cooked on their gas stove. I was never turned away or made to feel as if I had imposed upon their hospitality.

Lock and I both lived in the "country," like thousands of other Georgia boys reared in the '50s and '60s, with shared experiences of 'possum and squirrel huntin', frog giggin', fishin', haying, boxing, ramblin', and swimming in wash holes. We shared agrarian roots that transcended many generations; we were Southern bred and born; we were friends, neighbors, and teammates; our fathers were both educators; and even our birthdays were but a week apart. But for all of our similarities, Homer Lockwood had a unique feature that set him apart from my own background and that of many others: He was raised under the watchful care and influence of an extended family who lived all about him. His family of uncles, aunts, grannies, cousins, and, of course, his own mother and father, helped to raise him in the only home he had ever known—on the farm, under the traditions and lore passed down from centuries past.

But this book is not about Homer Lockwood. He has clearly stated that the main objective of this book is to honor and, in part, create a lasting memorial to the life of his daddy, Dean Myers. He nailed that objective with an eight-pound hammer! I am one of the many whose lives were impacted by Mr. Myers. I ate at his table, received his counsel, heard his storytelling, and was treated like his own son when I was blessed to work under his administration as a teacher in the school that bore his name. And I am convinced that at this very moment, Mr. Myers, as he watches with that great crowd of witnesses who have finished the race and now cheer us on from heaven, is proud of his son, Lockwood. This leaves the vast majority of the rest of us who have been blessed with a godly father just wishing we could honor our own with such a tribute.

Homer Lockwood is a true Southern humorist, and he comes by it honestly. His father could lead an audience from tranquil peace to absolute shock and terror within seconds when he abruptly concluded one of his famous yarns. Homer Lockwood, having received the gift, has caught the essence of the simpler time in which we grew up and the significance of our shared rural roots. He has captured the advantage received in experiencing living grandparents and wise old kinsmen who linked his life to an era that has passed us by; a time when the land was turned, the wagons were borne to the barn with power of the mule, and water was drawn from the well with a windlass and tin pail. Any Southern boy or girl—or, for that matter, anyone with rural associations—can relate with these experiences that Homer Lockwood has clearly laid out with enough nostalgia and feeling to bring back the memories. And even the urbanite who has never left the paved streets or manicured landscapes of the city can relish in the humor of the common human experience that is so well defined in these pages.

Famed Georgia humorist Lewis Grizzard wrote more than a few books with his Southern humor centered on his upbringing in a small Georgia town. It is my belief that Homer Lockwood has surpassed Grizzard and all the rest as he has drawn on his own raisin' in the North Georgia "country" that has now all but vanished. He is no Samuel Clemens—he did not grow up on the Mississippi—but he is Homer Lockwood Myers and, quite possibly to his advantage, does posses a distinct style of humor mixed with the insight and wisdom of Proverbs (and that of his own daddy), which has directed his life and makes reading this book a thoroughly enjoyable experience, not to mention the perfectly obvious source of the gift.

While I did laugh out loud on more than one occasion, the seriousness of Homer Lockwood's heart as he deals with issues such as "The Bandito," his relationship with his sister, Wyvonne, and several other touching subjects increases the depth of each of those matters. His handling of the distinguishing Southern trait of our carrying pocketknives is also insightful and right on the mark. But, in my opinion, he ends the book drawing on the best of his abilities and strengths. It is the perfect tribute to the father and friend of those lives who were, and are, better because they crossed paths with the life of an old hillbilly sharecropper teacher who more closely resembled the Carpenter of Nazareth than any other professional educator with whom it was my privilege to have been associated.

In conclusion, though Homer Lockwood is not the subject of this book, I believe it defines who he is and relates the source of the parts that make up the whole. Anyone who cannot find humor on every page should go ahead and make his or her prearranged funeral plans. This book is a good read, contains the mature wisdom of a life well lived throughout its pages, and chronicles the background of thousands of our generation. But, even more important for me, it is a tribute to a man that I loved and will always consider to be my "other father," Dean Myers, and it is written by a cherished friend with whom I share more than just a common generation.

—Ralph West Mills
Retired teacher and current cattle farmer

Introduction

IN 1974, AFTER graduating from North Georgia College with a stellar 2.000 GPA and serving a short stint in the U.S. Army as a dufus Second lieutenant, I began working as a life insurance agent. It was, as my mother-in-law put it, an okay position until I could find a real job.

A few years later, still not having found 8-to-5 employment, and actually beginning to be resigned to the possibility that selling life insurance might be my calling, I started a newsletter to send out to my clients—all three of them—and to my mother, sister, and any other relatives or friends who would let me put them on the mailing list. However, unlike the premade financial newsletters that no one read, I called on the memories of my childhood—from growing up on Granny England's farm to attending Candler Elementary where my daddy began his teaching career—for the material and articles in my bimonthly publication.

I used to get calls from people who had found the newsletter. People who had picked up a copy at the Longstreet Cafeteria (the best restaurant in the state of Georgia) or had been handed a copy by a friend or relative would call me to say that I was making a fool out of myself. Then they would tell me that as long as I was doing it anyway, I should put their brother, neighbor, pastor, and whoever else on the mailing list. As of this writing, the number of addresses on the mailing list for the newsletter has increased to more than 2,500. Not exactly the distribution of the *Wall Street Journal,* but okay for our little community.

The classroom was arranged in amphitheater style, even though it was indoors. When my dad, Dean Myers, and my uncle Bob Ables arrived (five minutes late), every seat was taken, except for a few on the front row. The professor had already begun the lecture.

The fact that they were late had been the center of a heated conversation between my dad and my uncle as they'd driven north up U.S. 441 through the Appalachian foothills to the campus of Piedmont College in the north Georgia town of Demorest. My dad was never late for anything. Bob was rarely on time, and when he was it was usually an accident.

Dad had repeatedly threatened to leave without him if he didn't find him waiting at the door. The two were making the three-days-a-week trip to the small mountain town campus to complete their two-year requirement for a teaching certificate, which both were pursuing while they worked full-time jobs. They were not only brothers-in-law but very close friends, which was one of the reasons Dad tolerated Bob's tardiness. The other reason was that they made a great team without even trying, which is usually the case with close friends.

Dad was tall and slender. Bob was about the same height, but he was...well, *robust.* My other uncle, Uncle Gene, my mom's brother, described them as a country bumpkin version of Stan Laurel and Oliver Hardy, but with reversed roles. My dad, a World War II veteran and sharecropper child of the Depression, was the straight guy; while Bob, who had grown up in the big city of Atlanta, was the one who always seemed to convince my dad to embark on some insane project. One time, he convinced Dad to burn off the brush behind our house, which turned into a full-fledged fire in the woods that required the turnout of all the neighborhood men to squelch. Apart they could both be considered normal, but together they were, as Gene put it, dangerous.

Acquiring the teaching certificate had been my dad's idea. He had used the G.I. Bill to underwrite most of the cost, and they had now been enrolled at Piedmont for almost two full years. So it was that they were nearing the end of their time there on that morning as they walked all the way to the front of the full classroom to claim two of the last remaining seats.

That's when Dad realized that in the rush he had forgotten to stop by the men's room to get rid of some of the coffee he had started drinking at 5:00 that morning. There was no way he was going to disrupt the class again and once more make a spectacle of himself by walking back up the aisle to the exit. Besides, it was 10:00, and the professor usually took a break at 11:00. So Dad just crossed his knees and decided to wait.

When the eleventh hour came and went, my dad realized that there would be no break. So he crossed his legs again and decided to endure the increasing discomfort until the lunch hour, when the class was scheduled to end. As the noon hour arrived—and passed—the biological alarm in his bladder began to sound in his brain.

Dad made the decision to get up and head to the bathroom. After exiting the men's room from down the hall, he saw that the long-winded professor was continuing to wax verbose. When he reached the double doors to the lecture hall, he stood there for a moment, trying to decide if he should even consider reentering. Just then, he noticed that he had left his trousers unzipped. As he attempted to zip up his pants, he kept his eyes focused on the classroom, which is why he never saw the woman with the wide dress coming.

The woman brushed by him and passed through the doors in such haste that she did not realize my dad had zipped her dress up in his zipper. In full stride, she carried him into the classroom, with my dad frantically shuffling behind her as he tried to dislodge the material of her skirt from his brass zipper.

This story has two endings, depending on who is telling it. Dad's version is that he was able to remove her skirt from his zipper without damage to him or her, with the exception of the humiliation, laughter, and resulting applause they received from the entire class as the lecture abruptly ended. Bob's version is that he was forced to offer the assistance of his pocketknife, without which the dress might have stayed caught in Dad's trousers until emergency help had arrived.

This story, like hundreds or perhaps even thousands like it, was told on the front porch of Granny England's house. The stories usually began after everyone had almost foundered on homemade ice cream or watermelon and had settled into the straight-back cane-bottom chairs or the rockers facing Candler road, which was paved in 1951, the year I was born.

By the way, in case you don't know what "foundered" means, it's when a horse (mules are too smart to founder) eats so much that his stomach expands and runs the risk of dying if he lies down. To prevent this, somebody—usually the person who left the lid off the sweet feed bin or the door open to the corn crib—has to stay up all night and walk him around the barn until the swelling in his stomach goes down. I won't go into what all is involved in the going down of the stomach process, except to say that it's a milder version of the Fourth of July fireworks and one should be outside while walking the horse.

Back to the stories. Most of them had some basis in truth or a factual starting point, but by the time the exaggeration and embellishment had been added…well, as Mark Twain said, the facts were never allowed to be a deterrent to a good story. If only I had had a tape recorder. What I wouldn't give to sit on that porch one more time with Gene, Uncle Bob Higgs, Gerald, Lamar, Bob Ables, and Daddy, just listening to them talk and tell stories.

We'd spend a summer evening watching the occasional car come down Candler Highway or the Gainesville Midland on its late-day run from Gainesville to Athens hauling cotton and cloth to and from the mills. For the most part the stories involved experiences of things that had happened to them, or perhaps a debate about whether red bones or black and tans made the best coon dogs. Between the stories, or during the ones that my cousins and I would not find interesting, we would run through the yard chasing lightning bugs or playing hide-and-seek.

This book is an accumulation of these types of stories from my newsletter. It is also a work done in memory of my daddy, who was a master storyteller and a remarkable man.

Welcome to *Homer's Porch*.

A 17-year-old Dean Myers stands beside a large gun on his ship.

Chapter 1

Family and Such

A good name is better than a fat bank account.
—Ecclesiastes 7:1, THE MESSAGE

There is transcendent power in a strong intergenerational family. An effectively interdependent family of children, parents, grandparents, aunts, uncles, and cousins can be a powerful force in helping people have a sense of who they are and where they came from and what they stand for.
—Steven Covey,
The Seven Habits of Highly Effective People

I PRINTED AND MAILED the first issue of the *Porch* in April 1999. In the March 2001 issue, I attempted to give a look into my mom and dad's people and the culture in the South. Here's how it ran in the *Porch*.

VIEW FROM THE PORCH

My wife, Renee, has been spending hours on the Internet researching our genealogy. Her efforts as a family tree detective have caused her to ignore her more important duties such as washing clothes, cooking, and such. When I humbly made mention of this, she

1

mumbled something like, "Go hire a maid, Shorty," and didn't even look up from the monitor. I might add that twice she has failed to complete the submissive wife course at our church.

However, I have found her thick notebook of research to be helpful in confirming or dispelling stories about my ancestors. For example, my grandfather Homer England, who is regularly featured on the front of this publication with me on his knee, supposedly had the required percentage of Cherokee to allow him to live on the reservation. His grandfather's tribal name was "He Who Tinkles with Forked Stream." There has always been a history of enlarged prostate in our bloodline.

But the volumes of Internet information my wife has collected have revealed something even more profound than the fact that our clan has a genetic inclination for staying in debt and stealing watermelons. What that research has revealed is that there is a difference between being a "redneck" and being "white trash." While our family has some of both in our pedigree, allow me to help *Porch* readers distinguish the difference:

1. My dad's people came from the mountains of eastern Tennessee and western North Carolina. Many of them made corn whiskey, which in those regions was considered to be an honest living, but also very redneck. When folks in that region drank too much corn whiskey and beat their wives and let their children go hungry…well, that was when they became white trash.

2. My grandmother Myers gave birth to fifteen children, a number not too uncommon for Depression-era farm families. That's redneck. However, none of those children was sired by his or her uncle or brother, which would've made them white trash.

3. Money does not elevate one from the ranks of redneckism. Case in point: My Uncle Gene England has made millions of dollars as one of the leading tractor dealers not only in the Southeast, but also in the entire country. He still wears white socks with his only blue suit to church on Sunday,

which makes him a redneck. However, he has not left his wife for a woman 30 years younger than him, nor has he unbuttoned his shirt to his navel and begun sporting a gold chain around his neck and blow-drying the hair on his chest. In other words, he's not white trash.

4. Holding political office also does not loosen the trappings of redneck culture. My dad was elected county school superintendent for three consecutive terms, but he continued to drive the same '64 Ford pickup to work for 12 years. That made him a redneck. However, he never had sex with a 20-year-old intern, which definitely would have made him white trash.

On Leave with Mom and Dad

After my father finished his two-year degree at Piedmont College, he found a job at Candler Elementary teaching science and math to sixth- through eighth-graders. He also drove a bus route, was one of two janitors at the school, and coached the boys and girls teams to several county basketball championships. On his off nights he would work a few hours at the A&P in Gainesville, but he had to reduce his time there when he was accepted to the University of Georgia (UGA). He eventually completed the requirements to earn his Ph.D., but he never received his doctorate because he was elected school superintendent and didn't have the time to write a dissertation.

During his first summer semester at UGA, he received notification that he would no longer be allowed to attend school there because he did not have a high school diploma. He had quit school in the fifth grade to work, as many other children had done during the Depression. As he drove home, he informed his carpool buddies that he was going to have to withdraw because of a lack of a high school diploma.

One of those buddies was the principal at North Habersham High School, which, even though it didn't exist during my dad's days, was located in the community where he grew up. This fellow was a free-spirit kind of guy and told my dad that he knew the solution to his problem and that he should keep attending UGA. When Dad got into the back seat of the car the next day at the rendezvous point for the carpool, his high-school principal buddy handed him a package containing a diploma of graduation for a high school that didn't even exist when Dad was of high-school age.

Reluctantly, and with a sense of guilt for which he never forgave himself, Dad delivered the diploma to the admissions office. Within a few days he was officially notified that his continued attendance had been approved.

My own college days were not nearly as demanding as my dad's, and I did not have the same perseverance that he had. Even though

4

he never brought it up, I knew there was no need to make excuses to him for my somewhat less-than-stellar performance in class. The June 2003 *Porch* gave some insight into my efforts during the five years I spent in college to earn my four-year degree.

VIEW FROM THE PORCH

North Georgia College was not exactly a hotbed of anti-establishment activism between the years 1969 to 1974, an era that included my not-so-distinguished attendance there. I graduated with a 2.0000 GPA and, even though North Georgia is considered (along with West Point and The Citadel) to be one of the top military schools in the country, my military bearing was lackluster.

Upon receiving my second lieutenant bars, a disgusted colonel stuck his finger in my chest and exclaimed, "Myers, you are bullet-stopping material, and I'm going to personally make sure that you go to Vietnam." Say what you want to about Richard Nixon, but he kept a bunch of bullet-stoppers like me from ending up face-down in a rice paddy.

Although North Georgia College may not hold the same stature as Harvard, I am proud and grateful to have graduated from there, even though it was by the skin of my teeth. However, not all my memories of my time there are pleasant, nor do I recall all of my professors with fondness.

One such professorette, who will remain nameless, was an early version of a militant feminist literature instructor who taught a course on the romantic era of culture and poetry. You might recall the period; it was dominated by names such as Wordsworth, Coleridge, and Lord Byron—the hippies of the 1800s. Their poetry and prose focused on the theme of the beauty of nature, including flowers, butterflies, green grass, and leafy trees.

After a few weeks, I found that I was the only male student left in the class. This became painfully obvious to me when one of my peers withdrew and told me how stupid I was for staying in a class with Ms. Professorette, who had a reputation for flunking male students. However, being the committed academic I was, and because my dad had told me that I would have to get a job if I dropped another class, I decided to attend each day, keep my mouth shut, and hope for the best.

Things proceeded well until about three weeks into the quarter. During one of Ms. Professorette's lectures—on the beauty of nature when undefiled by men—she turned to me and solicited my opinion on the subject. I don't know what came over me. Perhaps it was my redneck inner self wanting to break out and proclaim the truth, or perhaps it was the idea that some time off from school among the ranks of the gainfully employed wasn't such a bad idea after all. For whatever reason, I began to wax eloquent about the other side of nature, which I felt had been ignored up to that point in our class.

I proceeded to explain that although nature is indeed beautiful, it can also be horrific, like a bobcat ripping up a baby rabbit for breakfast or maggots roiling in a dead carcass. My oratory continued as I exclaimed that steam coming off fresh cow manure and sweat rolling off a mule's back were also nature in its rawest form. As I finished, I knew that I was in trouble because none of the coeds were looking at me. They were all staring at the floor, refusing to show any support for the condemned. However, the enlightened, open-minded, and above all *tolerant* professor was now standing with her arms folded, glaring at me. "Mr. Myers," she said, "you are very uncouth."

When the class was over, I went back to the dorm, found a dictionary and looked up "uncouth." That's when I decided to change from being an English major to majoring in business.

My subsequent years in the business department would prove to be every bit as challenging, but I had several great professors there. One was Dr. Larry Dennis, who personally tutored me and a few other dumb cadets through Accounting 101 and 102, which was something that probably would not have been done at some big state university.

Although I will not be remembered for my academic prowess at North Georgia, and I don't have enough money to leave the school to have a building named for me, I'm still proud of my old school and many of the men and women who graduated from there and distinguished themselves in service to our country.

My little sister, Sidney Wyvonne "Myers" Estes, was called by her second name, "Wyvonne," which came to be pronounced in our neck of the woods as "Y-vonne," the second syllable rhyming with *phone.*

When she was presented to me upon her arrival from the Hall County hospital maternity ward, I'm told that the first words out of my mouth were, "She looks dirty. Take her back." Two-year-olds don't have to worry about not expressing their true feelings. Maybe I felt a little threatened, having enjoyed the position of the first and only grandchild on my momma's side for the previous two years.

Family Camping Trip to Lake Vogel, North Georgia Mountains

My sister and I were never really close until about ten years ago, when she was around forty-five years of age. That's when, at the urging of our youngest son, Britt, I, along with my sister's husband, Ed, confronted her about her suspected drug addiction. Up until that point, even though we basically got along well—at a distance—I had pretty much taken her for granted.

The evening of the confrontation, she painfully confessed to having an addiction to prescription drugs, which she had obtained illegally. An addiction is an addiction regardless of the source of the substance used, but for those of us removed from the culture of the drug world, it's amazing how naïve we can be.

My sister's story has—and continues to have—a happy ending. When she emerged after six months of therapy and treatment, she asked me to make a deal with her that whenever the notion hit me, I could call her and ask her to go take a drug test. If she refused or made some excuse, then we both would know that she had returned to drugs. This arrangement has brought us much closer as brother and sister.

My sister came out of treatment in time for Christmas 2002. In the January '03 edition of the *Porch,* I finally gave her some credit for being a rich part of my life that I had heretofore always taken for granted.

VIEW FROM THE PORCH

Sisters are given to us boys for a good reason. Although I rarely say anything nice about mine, I have to confess that I've got a pretty good one. I enjoy introducing her as my older sister, even though she was born two years after me.

Her arrival was much less eventful to me than when we went to the Hall County Humane Society and I got my first dog, Flossie, who would stay my dog until my sophomore year in college. Flossie would also prove to be a lot less trouble to me and my childhood buddies who frequently visited our home.

We basically grew up on my grandmother England's farm, where the barn was the focal point of most of my daily activities. On some days the barn became the Alamo where my best friend,

J.W. Whitlow, and I, playing Davy Crockett and Daniel Boone, changed history and survived the battle against Santa Anna. Other times it served as a pirate ship or a great place to stage corncob battles or hide-and-seek as we scurried through the stables and stalls with other buddies in our farm community.

So it was with great trepidation that J.W. and I allowed Wyvonne to enter our sacred turf and join us on a great aeronautical experiment of jumping down from the barn loft using Momma's umbrella as a parachute. Even today, my sister twists the truth by alleging that we coerced her to go first, using her as a guinea pig test pilot. Not so. She insisted on going first, which, as budding southern gentlemen, we graciously allowed. Suffice it to say that J.W. and I decided not to follow suit after we witnessed the cloud of dust she created as the umbrella collapsed and her bottom splashed down in the barnyard. We also felt compelled to take the honorable course and report to Momma that it was Wyvonne who had torn up the umbrella.

On another occasion, Wyvonne insisted on intruding into a fun activity that J.W. and I had discovered. We would crawl into a 50-gallon barrel and, bracing our knees and elbows against the inside, would roll down a hill in the front yard, finally coming to a stop in a level pasture. (This was before the days of Game Boy.)

After enduring much pleading from Wyvonne, we held the barrel as she crawled inside and lay there limp like a house cat by the fire. She didn't ask for any advice, so we didn't offer any about how she should brace herself with her knees and elbows. As the barrel sped down the hill, she looked like one of those dice in a wire basket used in a lottery drawing. She emerged from the barrel with tangled blond hair and a bloody nose. Once she had regained her equilibrium, she chased us with a broken hoe handle to the refuge of the barn loft. We were safe there, since she had recently developed a fear of heights.

One of the most dastardly deeds she accused me and J.W. of doing was burning her at the stake. We were playing a game in which J.W. and I were the Apaches and she was a woman from a wagon train. It was our plan to change roles and be her rescuers, but we didn't expect the leaf fire to get out of control. Her singed eyebrows grew back long before the red stripes disappeared from my backside.

Although I participated in high school sports, I was never much of an athlete. I scored one touchdown during my senior year on an end sweep, but as I crossed the goal line I sucked a June bug down my throat that required medical attention while my teammates celebrated. Wyvonne, on the other hand, was a track and basketball star who on more than one occasion scored the last-second winning shot, which always caused my dad's eyes to water up. I'm convinced that much of the tenacity and aggressiveness that helped her to excel in athletics can be attributed to the attention and training that J.W. and I afforded her during her formative years.

Again, sisters are given to us boys for a good reason. With proper parenting, sisters teach us that boys are different than girls in ways that involve more than just the plumbing. They are to be respected and loved. It may be permissible to occasionally slug your brother, knowing that there will be consequences, but never your sister. Sisters are our equal in life and deserve every opportunity that boys are afforded, a concept promoted much more effectively by wise parents than a militant NOW.

Although the love we have for our sisters is different than the romantic affection we have for our wives, the respect and appreciation for the opposite sex can be greatly enhanced by learning how to love a sister. I'm grateful that I've got a great one.

The Soque River flows southeast into the great Chattahoochee River and then on into the Gulf of Mexico. But from its headwaters on the eastern slopes of the Appalachians extending into north Georgia from North Carolina, it is considered a mountain stream.

Each year, the Georgia Department of Natural Resources stocks about a mile of the river that is accessible to the public with hatchery

Homer's Grandparents and Two of His Father's 19 Siblings

trout. The remaining 15 or so miles of the Soque is bordered by private property, which a couple of northern Georgia outfitters lease and stock with trophy rainbows and browns. To fish this part of the river will run you around $300 a day, depending on which outfitter package you purchase.

My wife, who controls the finances in our house, lets me know without hesitation that the private part of the Soque is not in my fly-fishing budget. But, praise the Lord, I am blessed to have a good friend—who will remain anonymous so that none of my redneck friends who happen to read this (several of them can actually read) will start calling him—who allows me to fish on his stretch of the stream several times a year.

In addition to being a place for trophy trout fishing, the banks of the Soque and the mountain valleys it runs through have become second and, in some cases, first homes for many of the rich and affluent from Atlanta and other parts of the country. However, back in the 1930s and '40s, Georgia State Highway 197, which provides access to the Soque, was a graveled washboard road rather than the picturesque blacktop that parallels the stream today.

My dad and his 18 brothers and sisters were raised in a couple of sharecropper shanties, first on the White County side of the river and then later on the Habersham side, until Dad left home for the navy. I was probably about 10 years old when, as a side trip to our fishing outing, he drove down a nearly impassable washed-out side road to view the deserted, rusty, tin-roofed falling-in tenant house where much of his childhood had taken place. The rock chimney was the only part of the structure that seemed to be persevering against time and the elements. As we stood for a few silent moments in what had been his front yard, I'm sure I noticed his eyes getting a little watery. Then we left. That's when I began to figure out that his childhood had been a whole lot different than mine.

As Father's Day 2004 approached, I attempted to honor my dad in the following article from the *Porch* by showing readers the kind of wisdom and patience he had afforded to me as an impulsive and self-absorbed young man.

VIEW FROM THE PORCH

In the fall of 1968, pig prices were at their highest point in farming history. I know because I sold two prime porkers at the famous McEver's Meat Market in Talmo, Georgia, for 26 cents a pound on the hoof. The pigs were the result of a business endeavor that I had begun the previous March when I had purchased two shoats (adolescent piggies) from Mr. Phil Orr, a gentleman and farmer who was respected as much for his wisdom as his farming expertise.

Several of my friends and family scoffed when the news got out that I was getting into the pig business, but I didn't let this bother me. I knew that when I made the front page of the *Wall Street Journal* as the youngest pig tycoon in the southeast, they would see what a business prodigy I truly was.

The proceeds from the sale of the first two pigs provided just enough revenue to cover the previous six months' feed bill, for which my dad had unhesitatingly provided the financial underwriting. Even though I didn't earn a profit, I was not dismayed. I knew that next year would be better. I projected that not only would I cover the feed bill but that I would also pay for the cost of the fencing and such, and then I would expand by adding more pigs.

So, the following March, I purchased two more pigs from Mr. Orr, who allowed me to hold the eight-week-old piglets' hind legs while he castrated them then and there. Each day of the summer months that followed, I worked with a brick mason named A.J. Irvin, and when I got home in the afternoon I would feed and tend to my pork empire.

One experience that taught me an important (and almost costly) lesson was that one should never attempt to cool off a pig on a hot August day by squiring it in the face with a water hose. Fortunately, I was able to revive the pig after he passed out from the cold water hitting him between the eyes and save half of my herd. This may have been an omen for darker days ahead in the pig business.

Late into the summer, pig prices fell to 11 cents per pound, and a review of my books revealed that my empire was in trouble. I negotiated a chapter 11 bankruptcy deal with my banker (my dad), and he quietly took title to the pigs. They were quickly processed for home consumption, from which I still benefitted. My dad never said anything to me or anyone else about the stupidity of my pig endeavor, nor did he ever remind me of the loss. He just let me learn a painful lesson in Economics 101 about supply and demand.

For some reason, the memory of my pork debacle came to mind on this most recent Father's Day. As I recalled the patience and firm discipline my father demonstrated in raising me and my older sister, I wished I had used more of the same wisdom in raising our two sons, though—by the grace of God and a good mother—they have turned out pretty good in spite of my goofs.

My dad did not leave me a lot of material wealth. It never seemed important to him to accumulate it. But I did inherit his pocketknife collection, one of the few luxuries he allowed himself, and his '64 Ford truck, which he was driving to work the day he died. Of much more importance, what he did leave me was a priceless legacy that I confess I have tarnished at times. My prayer is that, in spite of my inconsistencies, I will be able to pass it on to my two sons.

Granny England's clapboard farm house, big barn, and other outbuildings, including the smokehouse and well house, were the settings for much of my childhood rompings and discoveries. One such memory about the well house, and an incident that occurred there when I was home one weekend from college, was the inspiration for an article that appeared in the November/December 2004 issue of the *Porch*.

VIEW FROM THE PORCH

There are two Geralds in our family (or at least there were—Big Gerald died a few years ago, but as of this writing, Little Gerald is still kicking). All families have characters, and ours has been blessed with an abundance of them. Big Gerald could have been best described as an Elvis clone with the toughness of a street fighter thrown in, while Little Gerald is more akin to Don Knotts (a.k.a. Barney Fife). Together they teamed up for many years to create stories that are still being told today.

Granny England's house was supplied with water from a hand-dug well. This well often collected frogs and other critters that met their demise from drowning in it, which left an unpleasant stench to the water. As a result, Big Gerald would often have to go down into the depths of the well to retrieve the offending carcass.

On one particular occasion, Big Gerald called me on a Friday night to enlist my help for the mission, which was scheduled for the following morning. When I arrived, Little Gerald was already on the scene giving directions and barking commands and, as usual, Big Gerald was ignoring him while attaching a World War I-era harness to the rafters of the well house. He had purchased the contraption of ropes and pulleys from the local navy/army surplus store, which was his favorite place to shop.

At first, the mission went well as Little Gerald and I commenced lowering Big Gerald into the dark depths of the well. But then, suddenly, we were besieged by a swarm of yellow jackets that one of us had unknowingly disturbed from their apartment complex under the concrete base of the well house. Little Gerald and I did what any caring and brave relative would do: We panicked, let go of the rope, and lit out for the refuge of the screen porch, fighting off yellow jackets as we ran.

Fortunately for Big Gerald, he had anticipated the unreliability of his helpers and had rigged the pulleys so that if we should let go of the ropes, the contraption would catch and not let him fall. Also fortunately for Big Gerald, the swarming bees did not descend into the dark well where he was suspended.

Little Gerald and I didn't know what to do, but finally we decided to wait on attempting a rescue until the yellow jackets settled down. When we were finally able to pull Big Gerald out, he was calmly smoking a Camel and had even been able to retrieve the dead frog.

Another uncle of mine was truly legendary in our parts. A man of good reputation, my Uncle Jack was probably in his eighties by the time I was old enough to know him. Of his many talents, some of the ones I was privileged to witness included shoeing mules, castrating pigs, and making flips (a forked stick with two straps of inner-tube rubber in between) for little boys.

Uncle Jack didn't wear boxer shorts or any other type of underwear under his overalls. This became public knowledge one day when he helped my father bore fencepost holes with an auger (a large drill on the back of a tractor). Like Bush Hogs and most other tractor attachments, the auger is extremely dangerous. If it catches a person's shirt sleeve or any other article of loose clothing, it can result in broken arms or worse.

I was busy defending the Alamo (Granny's barn) with my flip when I heard my mother screaming. Turning toward the commotion, I will never forget the scene I witnessed of my father sitting on the tractor with his mouth gaped open in shock, but relief, as an uninjured Uncle Jack watched his threadbare denim overalls spin tightly around the disengaged but still rotating auger. In an instant the machine had disrobed him, leaving him standing only in his brogans and felt work hat. Uncle Jack then did what any respectable 80-year-old farmer would do: He retrieved his pocket-knife from his shredded overalls, grinned at us, and calmly strode to the truck to wait until Momma brought him a pair of Dad's work trousers and a shirt.

By now you are probably wondering where I'm going with all of this. Well, there are some lessons to be learned here. First, don't stand too close to a spinning auger. Second, don't get all excited when you find yourself in an embarrassing situation over which you have no control. Finally, the next time you are abandoned by your friends and left suspended in a dark well, stay calm and hang in there—or get city water piped in.

Chapter 2

Lost Puppies and Such

Then the King will say, "I'm telling the solemn truth:
Whenever you did one of these things to someone overlooked or
ignored, that was me—you did it to me."
—Matthew 25:40, THE MESSAGE

M Y SISTER AND I were not allowed to say the *n*-word.
Although I will not claim purity of racial bias, I can't bring
myself to even type the word, because I know that somehow my
dad is quietly watching.

There was a nationally recognized, syndicated columnist by
the name of Ralph McGill who wrote for the *Atlanta Constitution/
Journal* in the '50s and '60s. My father was a big fan of Ralph McGill,
but many of the segregationists of the day were not. McGill was a
champion of integration before it was cool to do so. I can remember
hearing uncles, friends, and family members at family reunions and
"eating on the grounds"—outdoor church picnics—chide my dad
for his "*n*-lovin'" views.

Although people respected my dad, they definitely disagreed
with him and his admiration for McGill. In their view, blacks were to
be treated fairly as long as they "stayed in their place." "Separate but
equal" was the catchphrase that justified inferior school buildings

17

and white-only restaurants and most other public facilities in the community. However, the county and state courtroom was not separate and definitely not equal. Sadly, this phenomenon still exists today, with the most segregated institution being the church house.

Maybe it was because my dad had grown up so poor himself that he consistently found himself trying to help out folks whom you normally would not have invited home for Sunday dinner. (By the way, in the South, "dinner" refers to *lunch* and not the evening meal.) The first "lost sheep" that I can remember Daddy bringing to the house were a little boy and girl who were the children of a fellow he worked with at A&P, where he worked nights after teaching school all day. Their father had brought them to work with him that day and was planning on keeping them in the back of the store while he worked his shift.

Although the family was white, it was apparent to me and my sister that these kids were poorer than many of the black children we observed playing in the dilapidated playgrounds on the south side of town, and they seemed even poorer than the white children of the pulp wooding families that attended school with us. The best way I can describe them is to recall the scene in one of the film versions of *A Christmas Carol* by Dickens when the ghost of Christmas present opens his cloak and Scrooge is stunned by the shivering and emaciated boy and girl he sees before him.

Since we had already eaten supper with Dad, which we routinely did before he left for his second job, Momma quickly boiled some wieners and made hot dogs for the malnourished siblings. My sister and I watched in amazement as the little boy, probably about our age (six or seven), wolfed down six hot dogs, causing his stomach to actually protrude. I also remember Dad leaving to go back to work with one of those watery-eye looks he got from time to time. We continued to see our "Dickens children" for a season, about two or three nights each week while our fathers worked their night shifts at the A&P, and then they moved on.

Yet there was always a steady flow of other lost sheep who seemed to find their way to our house, or maybe Daddy just had a way of finding them. Either way, it was a part of my growing up. I would like to claim that it has made me more aware of the downtrodden and disadvantaged, but it really hasn't. Fortunately, I married a woman who is. The spring 2006 view from the *Porch* was an account of how big her heart really is.

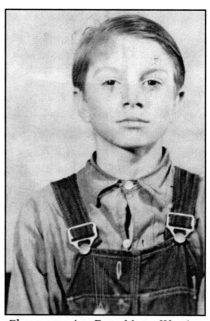

Elementary Age Dean Myers Wearing His Best "Sunday" Overalls

VIEW FROM THE PORCH

My wife, Renee, brought him home from school one afternoon, and he lived with us for almost a year. After retiring as an elementary school counselor, she had returned to a part-time status, working two days one week and three the next. Although we enjoyed the extra income, the real reason she went back to work was that she missed the kids. She had no problem filling her off-days with carousing with some of her other retired teaching buddies, shopping, and doing three-hour lunches, but she rebuffed any suggestions from me to take up a hobby and do something productive (like tying flies).

So, being of a little-better-than-average intelligence and being wise from working with children for more than thirty-five years, she must have known that his arrival in our house would change not only the routine of an empty-nest couple but also the schedule of Clyde, the spoiled overweight pug who thought we lived with him rather than the other way around. In my wife's view, the circumstances required immediate action.

The juvenile court judge, in an act that surpassed legal protocol and bureaucratic procedure, made a decision of the heart and assigned the boy's brothers and sisters to the homes of several teachers at the school and a pastor and wife in the community, who were all in the courtroom.

A year earlier, I had been severely scolded for allowing a stray dog that resembled a red Old Yeller to follow me home from jogging. I had offered the defense that I had not invited the dog to come home with me—he had just followed me there—but Renee just ignored me. She gave him a bowl of Clyde's gourmet doggy food and put down a blanket for him in the corner, protesting the whole time that we couldn't afford another dog. Since I had "found" him at my turnaround point at a railroad crossing, we named him Hobo, and he remains a part of the household today.

So it was with the same resoluteness that she brought the nine-year-old intruder to our roost. She says that she did ask me first, which really consisted of a phone call on the morning of the hearing to explain that the court had found homes for all of his brothers and sisters, and only he remained. And anyway, she added, it would just be for thirty days. I simply told her to do what she thought she should do, which, as I knew, she had already decided. The phone call to me was just a formality.

When I got home that evening, he stood at the kitchen sink with long unkempt hair and downcast eyes. The specific circumstances of his past were, sadly, not too uncommon for many children today. Without going into detail, suffice it to say that he and his siblings lived in filthy squalor and abuse.

It had been a while since a nine-year-old had been under our roof. Over the course of time, Renee taught him table manners, personal hygiene, and how to do math. For the first time in his life, he had a bedtime and a toothbrush.

Fern Patterson, a retired principal and fellow carouser with my wife who had grown up poor herself, gave hours of her life teaching him how to read. Other friends and family brought gifts to his birthday party and gave him attention. Although discipline had never been a problem with him, his whole demeanor began to change for the better. He began to talk—actually, he began to talk a lot, particularly when I was trying to read a book on the porch.

We took him on his first plane ride to Disney World and spent three days going on every ride in the place. I felt like I had run back-to-back marathons.

With the weight he had put on and his new haircut (I took him to a real barbershop), he was no longer recognizable by those who had seen him since his initial arrival. He enjoyed the children's ministry at church and started doing better in school. His improvement brought compliments to Renee and myself. Out of false modesty I disavowed much of the credit for his advancement, which my rude friend Les Johnson picked up on when he proclaimed, "Myers, all you've done is found somebody on your level to play with. Renee is doing all the work." And, truthfully, she was. From washing his clothes and helping him with homework, it was her routine and life that had been the most altered. Clyde and I just observed from the sidelines.

I will claim credit for teaching him how to whittle and trout fish. It took some time to convince him not to excitedly run up the river bank when he got one hooked and just reel it in, but he eventually got the hang of it. In fact, I have a picture in my office of him holding a fifteen-inch rainbow trout. I also taught him some other manly habits, like putting off scheduled chores to go fishing and peeing in the front yard after church. My retired pig-headed brother-in-law taught him how to argue. But, for the most part, Renee, the mother and teacher, brought discipline, order, and love into his life. He stole the hearts of several of our friends and, even though my brother-in-law won't admit it, he got to him too.

Inevitably, the time came for his departure. Renee and I had discussed and prayed about adopting him permanently, but it became apparent that we were just too old. Ultimately, it would have been be unfair to him. The original court order had been for thirty days, but a few days past a year, friends and family gathered at his favorite restaurant for a goodbye supper. Several of the women wiped tears from their eyes, and a few of the men discreetly excused themselves to the men's room to get "squared away."

But this story has a happy ending. In answer to our prayers and the prayers of many of our friends, he was accepted into

Chick-fil-A's WinShape Homes for children. Not only would this provide a loving environment for him, but he would also be joined with his brothers and sister.

We drove him there one Saturday morning. I had resolved not to make a slobbering, sniffling fool out of myself. Well, so much for resolve. Even the seasoned veteran school counselor, who had witnessed hundreds of traumatic events in other children's lives, didn't handle it as well as I had anticipated. But we both kept it together well enough to wave good-bye and force a smile through our tears as we drove away, leaving a significant chapter of our lives behind.

Today, he and his siblings are thriving in a loving home and are attending an excellent private school provided through a wonderful ministry. I had given him a nickname early on as "The Bandito," translated as the Bandit. Of course, he was not a bandit, but it was one of the few Spanish words I knew. Little did I know at the time how appropriate it would become, because Geraldo "The Bandito" Jimenez did indeed steal our hearts.

Geraldo "Bandito" Jimenez

Much to the consternation of my mother, who believed in sterile housekeeping and tidy yards, Daddy loved dogs, and he handed the gene down to my sister and me. I knew that he would usually give permission for me to bring home most of the stray dogs that were dumped out on the gravel road we lived on or that just showed up at our back door. Sometimes we actually found permanent placement for the homeless pooches, and sometimes they ended up with us.

The dogs that became part of my growing-up days included "Sam," a gentle boxer; "Blue," a hound that would eat sliced tomatoes and anything else raked out from our kitchen; "Bird," a long-haired bird dog that would hunt and tree possums but not hurt them; and, finally, "Flossie," a cocker spaniel whose lifespan spread from my second-grade year to my sophomore year in college.

That I transitioned into adulthood with this canine weakness would have been okay except for the fact that I married a woman who was, and continues to be, more afflicted with it than I am. The May/June 2000 *View from the Porch* illustrated how bad the problem had become.

VIEW FROM THE PORCH

We received some discouraging news last week. Renee returned home from the vet's office to report that Clyde, our dog, would be henceforth restricted to a rigorous diet—no more marshmallows or Slim Jims. Clyde is a pug, and if you are unfamiliar with the short stocky breed, they resemble a fat Beagle with shorter ears and a smushed-up nose that looks like it rear-ended a brick wall at a high rate of speed. The breed's attributes include loud snoring, twelve months of continuous hair shedding, and gastrointestinal eruptions, usually timed when guests are over.

The diagnosis came from our vet and my fly-fishing partner, Dr. Ed "Quack" Quillian, who was considering the cost of a new fly rod when he sold Renee some expensive doggy diet food as she left his office. Renee has been convinced that Dr. Ed is an excellent vet ever since he conjured a wart off of Clyde's ear. Clyde, who tipped the scales right at thirty-five pounds (his suggested body weight is twenty-two pounds), doesn't share Renee's regard for the vet, and especially the recommended diet.

According to the diagnosis, Clyde was to embark on a high-protein diet that resembled freeze-dried red worms. Clyde would have rather had his hind leg amputated than eat freeze-dried red worms. He took the news hard and overdosed on an entire pack of Fig Newtons (his favorite cookie) that he managed to steal from the pantry, and then spent the rest of the evening comatose and pouting under our bed.

The next day, Renee and Clyde visited our local chain pet store, where they let you bring your dog inside but your kids have to stay in the car with the windows up. As they were riding through the checkout line in a buggy (Clyde thinks that walking is overrated), he spotted a Bar-BQ pig ear, his favorite treat. Renee, who was supposed to be resolute in committing Clyde to his diet, succumbed to his wailing and gnashing of teeth and bought him the pig ear.

That was when she heard a woman behind her curtly offer the comment, "Your dog is too fat." When Renee turned to view the source of the scolding, she saw a Woody Allen-looking woman wearing a PETA tank top shirt and sporting a NOW tattoo on her shoulder. PETA (People for the Ethical Treatment of Animals) is the organization that recently declared the milking of cows to be animal cruelty. Having grown up on a farm, I don't think they have ever asked a cow that is overdue to be milked about that…, but I digress.

PETA woman continued her public reprimanding by likening Renee's allowing Clyde to become obese to torture or even murder. As Renee reached into her purse for her car keys, she promptly told PETA gal to mind her own business, and then threw another pig ear into the buggy. All the commotion and excitement so upset Clyde that he began to experience gastrointestinal eruptions to the extent that it sent PETA woman and several other customers rushing to the exits.

Renee still plans to keep Clyde on his diet. No more Fig Newtons or Mayfield Moose Track ice cream. Too bad dogs can't smoke. His food intake is supposed to be limited to about 500 calories per day, about the same as that of children living in poverty-stricken areas of the Earth's third-world countries. Wonder if PETA has any chapters there.

Clyde

There probably could not have been a more appropriate community school for my father to begin his teaching career than Candler Elementary. The original red brick building, located in the rural southeastern section of Hall County, Georgia, was named after a former governor of the state. When Dean D. Myers, a skinny version of Andy Griffith with some Ichabod Crane oddities thrown in, started his career in education there, no one, especially him, ever suspected that the school would one day be renamed in his honor.

By the time I attended Candler Elementary, a new building that housed the principal's office and three new classrooms with electric heat and indoor restrooms had been added. However, my dad's first classroom assignment was in the original wood-floored, square red-brick building. It was heated by four large coal-fed heaters, which would glow red in the winter months. A boys' and girls' outhouse was maintained at the edge of the playground, which consisted of several sets of swings, a sliding board, a see-saw, ten-plus acres of woods, and a grassy area for softball games. The wooded area provided the turf for unstructured recess games of fox and hound, hide-and-seek, and fighting, which, along with bloody noses and black eyes, was said to build character.

I gave readers a glimpse of a day at Candler Elementary in a July/August issue of the *Porch*.

VIEW FROM THE PORCH

Childhood isn't simple anymore. Maybe it never was, but it sure seemed a lot simpler to me when I was growing up in the Candler community of Hall County, Georgia. Hall, and the county seat of Gainesville, is about 40 miles north of Atlanta, right about where the hills start that soon become the southernmost end of the Appalachian mountain chain as one travels north.

Gainesville was a small town with a big town attitude, but the culture and demographics of the Candler community was definitely rural. In the '50s, Candler was a blue collar community where folks still tended a garden with a mule rather than a garden tiller. Entertainment included attending all night gospel "sangins," watching *Bonanza* and *Gunsmoke* along with *The Andy Griffith Show*, and going to the Royal Theatre on Main Street in downtown Gainesville on Saturday afternoon.

I attended Candler Elementary School. Instead of a structured PE class, we had recess, which was much more educational because it provided an opportunity to learn important social skills like fist-fighting and cussing. My best friend at Candler was J.W. Whitlow.

J.W. had a speech impediment (we simply described it as "he can't talk plain"), which made him the target of just enough abuse to get us both into fights. However, even though I suffered numerous nosebleeds and black eyes, my parents rarely had to get involved or worry about me being shot or stabbed by a gang member.

The most dangerous person in the entire school was Montine Crotwell, a girl who had six toes on each foot and five fingers and a thumb on each hand. Montine was in our fourth-grade class, but she could whup up any boy through the sixth grade, and most of the seventh- and eighth-graders knew to leave her alone. She could throw and hit a softball farther than anyone and could outrun all of us.

One time, she caught J.W. staring at her toes in the lunch room (we usually went barefoot to school in the late summer and late spring months of school) and threatened to beat him until he could talk plain. Out of sheer fright, I pleaded with her to let J.W. go, and, surprisingly, she did. This was quite out of character for Montine, because she took great offense to folks looking at her toes.

Another friend of ours, who was equally scared of her, was so impressed by my oratory and gift of persuasion that he said I should be a TV preacher or a salesman when I grew up. I opted for the latter because I don't like hair spray. I never told our friend that the real reason Montine let J.W. off the hook was because I promised her my orange push-up ice cream at the next snack break.

If anyone could have inflicted more pain than Montine, it was our fourth-grade teacher, Ms. (The Inquisitor) Snodgrass. There was a fat (obesity-challenged) kid named Eddie in our class who was always betting or daring someone to do something stupid. One day during recess, Eddie dared J.W., who had drawn Montine's name for the Christmas gift exchange, to give her a pair of gloves. God had given J.W. just average intelligence, but he knew enough to realize that such an act would lead to pain and suffering at Montine's hands.

God had also given J.W. and me a born immunity to poison oak and ivy, which grew plentifully around the playground. We both took great pride in this, because we figured it gave us a genetic link to Davy Crockett and Daniel Boone, whom we were sure had been immune to the evil weed as well. Eddie, however, did not share our immunity to the cursed sumac, so when we proceeded to pull and rub some on our hands and face and dare him to do the same, he couldn't resist. We didn't see Eddie at school for several days after that, but when he did return, his head was still swollen over his ears.

When The Inquisitor found out my and J.W.'s involvement in the matter, we tried to offer the defense that we were only trying to save Eddie from a life of gambling, but this didn't save our back ends from experiencing the wrath of God. No counseling. No discussion or parent complaints. Just two sore rear ends and two wiser young men.

J.W. lived in an old, clapboard two-story house. It had long been abandoned by its former charm, and one of the floors in a bottom room had rotted out. His dad was a pulp wooder and would often bring J.W. and his sisters to school in the pulp wood truck when the dirt road they lived on was too muddy and impassable for the school bus.

I loved to spend the night with J.W. because we could play in the room with the dirt floor. My mother was a little uneasy at first about me going home with J.W., but my father reassured her that J.W.'s dad was a hardworking man and that his parents were good folks. There were no rich kids in our class, and the gap between the haves and have-nots was narrow and almost indistinguishable. Even though the community was mostly lower income, I don't recall any of my friends coming to school hungry or with cigarette burns or hearing about anyone who had suffered sexual or emotional abuse.

Matt Dillon dispatched bad guys on *Gunsmoke* when he had to do so, but he didn't blow them away and splatter their blood all over the TV screen. I hunted squirrel with my older uncles and was allowed to shoot a .22 rifle when I was ten years old, but I never considered shooting my classmates. I know that life wasn't as innocent as I remember it, and I'm not suggesting that every moment of my childhood was a Norman Rockwell moment. Perhaps we simply choose to forget the ugly stuff. But I do know that I had two parents who loved me and that I was surrounded by family who helped get me to adulthood, which seems to work a lot better than family and children services doing it or being raised by the "village."

Perhaps there is something to what people like Dr. James Dobson, founder of Focus on the Family, has been saying all along: The originator of the concept of family also has the best advice on how family should be practiced and lived.

Although I'm sure they existed, I don't remember seeing any day cares when I was growing up or recall any of my friends staying in one. I know that there are some well-run ones today and that many single moms and working parents have no other alternative but to put their kids in one. Maybe I just wasn't paying attention, but it seems that day care, just like homes for the elderly, was a concept that was just getting started while I was growing up.

For centuries prior, humans had, for the most part, raised their children at home and kept their aging parents with them until death. Fortunately for me and my Grandmother England, we both came along at a time when the young and aged were provided with a place to be—in my case for all of my childhood, and in her case until her death. That place was her farm and the farmhouse where she'd given birth to nine children and raised them "out of the house" to lead productive lives.

I recalled some of my memories of spending my days at Granny England's house in the Christmas 2006 issue of the *Porch*.

VIEW FROM THE PORCH

My Granny England maintained a two-mule farm for several years after the death of her brick mason/farmer husband, my grandfather Homer England. Although the farm did not prove to be economically efficient, it provided her with a sufficient livelihood until her last child moved out. It also provided me with a childhood experience that only a few of my aging Baby Boomer peers can claim.

Our house was connected to Granny's by only 100 yards of old abandoned county road, but that road connected me to a world of woodstove heat, fall hog killings, plowing the bottom land with a mule, and a host of other experiences that were unique to farm life. I traveled the road to Granny's each day until my high school activities, more social than academic, became a priority. Yet I never appreciated the times I spent there until much later in life, well after Granny was gone.

All four seasons had their unique activities, but Christmas was my favorite time on the farm. Granny had electricity by the time I came along, but the primary source of heat was a pot-belly heater in the dining room and an open fireplace in the living room. She only reluctantly replaced her wood cook stove, on which she cooked three meals a day, with an electric range when I started the fifth grade.

The main bedroom was not heated, and it was there, under her bed, that she stored boxes of peppermint candy and chocolate drops along with the season's supply of apples and navel oranges. (My Uncle Gerald, who taught me how to sharpen a pocketknife, would use his knife to cut a hole in one of the big navel oranges and then insert a peppermint stick for me to siphon out the juice.) Overnight stays, which were frequent for me, meant sleeping in one of the smaller beds with eight to ten blankets stacked on top. My older (and spoiled) sister slept with Granny under an electric blanket.

Santa Claus came to our house sometime after bedtime on Christmas Eve, so it wasn't hard for my parents to get me home. But after we had opened the gifts under our tree, it was just understood that we would be spending a good part of Christmas Day at Granny's. One year, tragedy struck when my Uncle Gene accidentally allowed one of his coonhounds to get a hold of a new Davy Crockett coonskin cap that I had received as a present. The cap was quickly replaced the next morning when the stores reopened, and Granny proceeded to beat Gene over the head and shoulders with a broom handle.

After Christmas break during my fourth-grade year, several of the boys in my class, including me, returned to school with gun replicas of our favorite TV Western show heroes. Matt Dillon (*Gunsmoke*), Paladin (*Have Gun–Will Travel*) and Chuck Conner (*The Rifleman*) were well represented by those of us who were fortunate to get a gun replica for Christmas. One year, the only rich kid in our class (at least we thought he was rich because his momma brought him to school in a Cadillac) got a much sought-after, expensive, and hard-to-find toy replica of Steve McQueen's short barreled shotgun. J.W. and I had coveted that gun, but we had known not to ask for it because it was too expensive.

Of course, times have changed, and today kids are never allowed to bring toy guns to school. A few years back, I served two terms on our county school board, which was more than long enough to realize how easy it is to make enemies quickly while in elected office—especially when you are on the local school board. Many of the decisions we made were simple, but one of the most difficult ones that I ever had to vote on was to uphold the decision to suspend a fourth-grader for bringing a toy gun to school. Somehow, I felt the guilt of hypocrisy as I voted with my peers to send the little fellow home for the remainder of the school year. But, in the simpler days of my elementary school years, the thought of kids showing up at school with real guns and shooting their classmates and themselves was unfathomable. (Regardless of which side of the gun debate you are on, I think we all would agree that the cause of these kinds of tragic school shootings are complex and don't start with toy guns.)

That same year, several of our girl classmates returned to class with their first bras. If you are a fourth-grade boy and witness a fourth-grade girl go from being flat-chested to a size A in just two weeks during the Christmas break, it should get your attention. But me, J.W., and the rest of my buddies were more interested in what toy gun or bone-handled Case pocketknife had been left under the tree.

One person who did notice was Mr. Rich Kid. As he operated his lever-action Steve McQueen gun, he gave us an assessment of all the new bras on the girls in school and mentioned that Montine Crotwell, who came from a poor family, had not received one. He added that she was so flat-chested that she probably wouldn't need one until she was an old woman—like age 25 or so.

As I mentioned previously, Montine was the meanest and toughest kid in our school. Unbeknownst to Rich Kid, she happened to be walking by behind him as he made his comment about her lack of a bra or need for one. Apparently, this had already become a sensitive issue for Montine, and just as Rich Kid stopped laughing at his own joke about her, he turned and saw her quickly approaching with her fist balled up. In his panic he ran with the speed of a gazelle, but Montine could run like a cheetah and soon caught him in the far corner of the playground, where she proceeded to break his Steve McQueen gun over his head. So much for the theory of the weaker sex being weaker.

There would be a few more Christmas memories made at Candler Elementary and at Granny's house, and I naïvely assumed that those days would never end. But they did, and sooner than I could have imagined. Now those Norman Rockwell images only dimly exist only in the back corners of my mind, which makes me even more grateful for them.

My father didn't mean to get himself elected county school superintendent, but it happened anyway. It came about when a bunch of county residents met to discuss a school crisis and the unwise leadership they determined was being provided. Someone suggested collecting funds to remedy the situation and, once it was collected, someone else suggested that the money be used to fund the campaign for Dean Myers to assume the superintendent's job.

Dad was fired the next morning, but he was elected school superintendent that fall. That was in 1968, the beginning of my senior year in high school. I remember it well because later that year, Mrs. Peggy Hall, our physics teacher, said to me, "Homer, it's going to be embarrassing when your daddy is handing out diplomas next spring and you don't get one." So much for positive reinforcement.

Once Dad took office, he found himself being courted by bankers, who wanted to set up accounts for the school system's money; other local politicians, who wanted to form alliances with him; and sundry other community movers-and-shakers, who wanted to build or protect their own turf. One of those movers-and-shakers was a woman whom we will call Jezebel, so as to protect the guilty. Jezebel was an attractive woman who had reportedly used her feminine charms to convince a congressman to place her in charge of an entitlement program left over from LBJ's "Great Society" (which, incidentally, worked out as about as well as LBJ holding his beagle by its ears). Jezebel was quite the politician and had a handpicked board of directors that included whoever held the school superintendent job.

This had been working out well for her until a country boy hillbilly in the person of my dad filled the slot. Dad was not necessarily outspoken, unless he perceived that someone was trying to take advantage of the disadvantaged or defenseless. This he soon did after attending his first board meeting with all of Jezebel's "yes" board members, who never questioned any of her decisions—particularly those about money.

Integration was being implemented in the country's public schools at the time, and though it was a non-event locally due to the influence of some black pastors and businesspeople, it (along with managing the affairs of a rapidly growing school system) made Dad plenty busy. So when word got back to him that Jezebel had labeled him a "hayseed bigot" for questioning her handling of finances and federal grants, Dad resigned her board and gave his full attention to the school system.

Fast-forward a couple of years later to a spring day in downtown Gainesville, Georgia, when a bunch of FBI agents showed up at the offices of Jezebel and company and proceeded to put padlocks on all her files and handcuffs on many of the staff—including ol' Jez as well. It seems that a disgruntled employee had tipped the

G-men off that Jez was skimming money off the top of one of the grants specifically aimed at inner-city poor children.

When it was all over, the only thing I remember my dad saying about it was, "Liberals love to 'love' other people with other people's money." Maybe that's why the kid mentioned in the January/February 2008 issue of the *Porch* came to my attention.

Superintendent of Schools, Dean Myers, with Transportation Staff and Drivers

VIEW FROM THE PORCH

On the way to the office the other day, I noticed a kid at a broken-down swing set on the "playground" of one of the government housing projects in our small town. As I sat through the long red light, he stood out because he appeared much bigger than the other five- and six-year-olds who scurried around the dilapidated playground equipment. Maybe he was just big for his age, but for some reason I suspected that he was a very bored nine- or ten-year-old with nothing much else to do.

The scene caused me to recall, with thanksgiving and appreciation, my own childhood and many of the options I had at the start of each day. This is not to suggest that I led a life without bumps, but whether I was in school or out, I always had a number of potential activities to choose from at the beginning of each day. Even though I had to deal with arithmetic and bullies when school was in session, there was always recess—a time when me and J.W. Whitlow and some of my other buddies would take Iwo Jima or defend the Alamo.

I always got off the bus at Granny England's house and, after wolfing down one of her leftover cat-head biscuits from breakfast as an after-school snack, I would usually team up with Tommy Purcell from just down the road. We would roam the surrounding woods or play in the barn until suppertime. The only risk that threatened our play activities was if Uncle Gene conscripted us into following him and Kate, the mule, to the bottoms where we were required to strow guaner (scatter fertilizer) in the plowed rows or split pine slats into wood for Granny's stove. When we escaped Uncle Gene, which we usually did, we built teepees on the open plains of the pasture and made bows and arrows from hickory limbs with our own pocketknives, which no one ever questioned us carrying. When we were tired of defending the Alamo or fighting the Japanese Imperial Army, we could dam up the Walnut River or even venture to the Calvary Hole a little farther upstream where the Calvary Baptist church held their baptisms.

Although TV viewing was a limited part of our routine, Saturday programming included classic comedy shows starring The Three Stooges or Laurel and Hardy. A "ghost" movie came on in the early afternoon featuring greats like Bela Legosi as count Dracula or Boris Karloff as Frankenstein, who, by the way, teamed up with the greatest comedy team of all time to make the classic *Bud Abbott and Lou Costello Meet Frankenstein.*

During baseball season, Dizzy Dean was the color man for Peewee Reese as they did the game of the week. Diz, who was a native of Arkansas and would enter Major League Baseball's Hall of Fame as one of the sport's greatest pitchers, was a natural born humorist who didn't come close to resembling the loudmouthed abrasive sports analysts of today.

On Sunday afternoons, Johnny Unitas threw darts to flanker Raymond Berry, while Bart Starr drove the Packers. Both all-pro quarterbacks guided their teams to championships. And Jim Brown, who looked as if he could barely make it back to the huddle, would come out and glide down the field to score countless touchdowns. However, to my knowledge, none of them used any "substance" to enhance their performance or danced in the end zone to taunt the opposition.

Of course, life wasn't perfect. Some of our peers were neglected or even abused, and the threat of atomic bombs meant that fallout shelters were part of our childhood reality.

As the light turned green and the playground slowly disappeared in my rearview mirror, I watched the big kid idly passing the day away and wondered what I would have done if I were in his place. Would I have had the discipline to resist the temptations of using drugs or joining a gang? Would I have had the resilience to survive the abuse he probably faced each day? I quickly concluded I probably would not have, and I silently offered a prayer of gratitude for my childhood and a prayer of hope for the future of his.

Chapter 3

Education and Work

Do you see a man skilled in his work? He will stand before kings;
he will not stand before obscure men.
—Proverbs 22:29, NASB

So I hated life, for the work which had been done under
the sun was grievous to me; because everything is
futility and striving after wind.
—Ecclesiastes 2:17, NASB

WHEN I LEFT Fort Benning in the spring of 1974, the country was in the midst of the most severe economic downturn since the Great Depression. My second lieutenant pay was just a shade over $9,200 per year, but my plan was to return to Hall County and work with A.J. Irvin, a brick mason who had been my employer every summer of my high school and college years. The pay was a little more than what the army was paying, but the problem was that there was not a lot of brick being laid or much of anything in the way of job opportunities for a C-student with a general business degree whose only skills were making mortar and building scaffolds.

A.J. Irvin had raised and college-educated three daughters, and he had a poultry farm that more than maintained his and his wife's standard of living. Even though he didn't have to keep bricking houses to eat, he was still committed to employing Don Cooper, a young man about my same age, who had worked with A.J. year-round. Because I had a college education, A.J. suggested I go find a profession outside of masonry. This might have also had something to do with my brick mason skills, which he had let me try on the days that I got ahead with making mortar.

Several banks offered me employment as a general flunky to see if I had any potential. In addition, because my dad was a well-respected educator by this time, some friends and relatives assumed I would go into teaching. But I wasn't banking material, and I wasn't teaching material, either.

My Uncle Bob Higgs was an actuary for a small life insurance company domiciled in Atlanta, and on one of his visits to our house he suggested that I might consider the life insurance sales profession. "You have the gift of gab with some horse manure thrown in," he said. "Plus, some of our top salesmen make more than our company president." That was all I needed to hear, especially the part about making money. So, with this noble motivation, I walked into the offices of Metropolitan Life in downtown Gainesville and asked for a job in sales.

One year later, after qualifying for the company's sales convention (which resulted in my walking around the office with my nose up in the air), the sales manager finally told me that the only reason he had hired me was because he was under pressure to hire two new people each month. I was his last choice out of fifteen people who had been recruited and had turned him down. This didn't do much for my self-esteem, but it did help improve my pompous posture.

But, thirty-five years later, I can look back and conclude that I probably have been blessed to be in a business that, even though I threatened to quit on numerous occasions, has been a good place for me. However, the best job I ever had came long before I entered the life insurance business. I had a chance to tell about it in the September/October 1999 issue of the *Porch*.

VIEW FROM THE PORCH

The best job I ever had was working with my Uncle Gene on his milk route when I was in the fourth and fifth grades. Gene would go on to become one of the leading dealers for a major tractor company, but his first public job off the farm was running a milk route for one of the local dairies. We delivered milk in cold glass jugs to back porches and small grocery stores on the south side of town that have since been erased by urban renewal. Gene paid me five dollars per day, two more than the going rate for milk boys, and gave me all the chocolate milk I could drink.

Our day began around 4:00 AM, and after a few stops we would end up at Zeke's Pancake House around 6:00. After a plate of pancakes and sausage, we ran hard until about 1:00 PM, which was when the lunch crowd started thinning out at Mr. McNeal's, who served the best fried chicken in the western hemisphere. Mr. McNeal had the largest following on Sunday after church (Baptist), which just confirmed that his fried chicken was special.

Our last stop, and the climax of the day, was at a business that had outlived its time but was still in operation in the late '50s: Bagwell's Mule Barn. The Bagwell brothers ran this mule barn where customers, along with buying mules and farm implements, traded pocketknives and gossiped or just sat and whittled. My first task upon arrival was to put new bottles of milk in the RC Cola icebox, which sat in a small office over in the corner of the huge barn. There were some other bottles of clear liquid that Gene never got around to telling me about, though it seemed to disappear a lot faster than the milk.

The décor in the small office was unique. *Playboy* pin-ups covered every inch of the wall space and the ceiling except on one wall, where a portrait of one of Georgia's most notorious governors and segregationists, Gene Talmadge, was hung. The artist had painted Governor Gene wearing a dark blue suit and holding his hand on the Bible, which to me always seemed to contrast with the pin-up girls. All of it together was a sight to make a nine-year-old boy's mouth drop open. Plus, it was my first exposure to a real Democrat.

Like most boys, I had other jobs, like slinging weeds off the church cemetery for Mr. Carlton Land. Mr. Carlton drove a school bus for forty years without an accident, which could partly be attributed to the fact that he never changed out of second gear. Kids and parents alike loved him, but you sure didn't want to get behind his bus if you were in a hurry.

The summer before my ninth grade year, my father introduced me to A.J. Irvin, which would prove to be a defining moment in my life. A.J. was a World War II veteran who resembled a blend of Clint Eastwood and John Wayne. By the time I came to be one of his employees, two major events had tamed him somewhat: his encounter with Jesus Christ and his marriage to Flora.

My first day on the job, we were bricking a house that sat on a steep slope that quickly dropped off to Lake Lanier. A.J. had instructed me not to overfill the wheelbarrow with mortar until I got used to handling it. However, anxious to impress him, I filled it to capacity and headed downhill to the rear of the house, where A.J. and another mason were working from the top of a scaffold. But instead of making the 90-degree turn to where they were working, I followed the wheelbarrow…right into the lake.

Although I had managed to keep the wheelbarrow from turning over, it was completely submerged, and I stood in the water about waist deep. After I had stood there tightly gripping the handlebars for what seemed like a long time, A.J. calmly turned in my direction and said, "Son, I believe that mortar is a little too wet." To my surprise and relief, he didn't fire me. But years later when he told the story, he admitted that it was hard for him to not laugh. I would work for him for eight more summers, learning a good work ethic and lessons about life.

Today, as I see kids sucking in the sewage of MTV and joining gangs and such, I'm convinced that another government-funded organized sports program—or any government program, for that matter—is not the solution. Many of them need a JOB. And not just any job, but one that comes with the influence of men like my Uncle Gene, Mr. Carlton Land, and A.J. Irvin to help mold their lives and character.

About 30 years ago, during a short business trip to Savannah, Georgia, my schoolteacher wife, Renee, had conscripted me into following her through the many gift shops that line River Street. I would rather have been playing tennis, but since I had played the previous two days during the afternoon breakouts from the meeting, I knew that there were privileges to lose if did not opt for the shopping.

I prefer getting my teeth cleaned to shopping, but I actually found myself enjoying the afternoon as I observed all the activity on the oldest street of one of the oldest cities in the country. I found a coffee house and was content to munch on a honey oatmeal raision cookie and sip a cup of dark roast coffee while Renee went in and out of the gift shops, picking up and turning over every piece of merchandise in the stores without buying a thing. The primary reason she was not making any purchases had something to do with our limited budget at the time, but still, she was just content to shop and give the store clerks something to do by rearranging everything after she finished.

About the time I finished the cookie, she summoned me into one of the shops to show me a sculpture she had found. My taste in art is akin to neoclassic white trash, and the only sculpture I had ever stopped more than 30 seconds to look at was the carving of the confederate generals on the granite face of Stone Mountain. As I followed her to the corner of the shop, she picked up and held out a figure of what was instantly recognizable as a schoolteacher. The artist was one Tom Clark, and the work was titled "Miss Mary." Attached to the base beside Miss Mary was an antique school desk. Miss Mary held a pencil and a writing slate in her hands, but it was her face that really grabbed you. It reflected wisdom combined with kindness as she appeared to be standing before her classroom, which was filled with students.

Renee turned the piece over to reveal the price tag stuck on the bottom: $300. Without saying a word, she set it back on the shelf, and we went back to our hotel to get ready for dinner. Even though nothing had been said, I knew she really wanted the limited-edition rendition of the aging teacher.

I turned on the TV to get the weekend football scores and to get Miss Mary off my mind, but I couldn't. I had been pigeonholing some cash to buy a new scope for my deer rifle, and the amount happened to be in the denomination of three $100 bills hidden behind my driver's license in the recesses of my wallet. When Renee got into the shower, I left the room and returned to the shop. In probably the only romantic act of our marriage, I traded my three "Benjamins" for Miss Mary. The shop owner must have perceived my limited finances, as he threw in the sales tax for free.

Since then, Miss Mary has held her place on a coffee table in our den with silent dignity while surviving two boys growing up in the house and their collection of rambunctious friends. It's amazing how much Renee's face has come to resemble Miss Mary's in recent years. I guess thirty-five years of teaching and counseling kids, their parents, and even her peers on the faculty have a way of doing that.

Although I claim no expertise in offering any solutions to our education problems, I have observed several fine educators, along with Renee and my father, who have the authority to address the subject. This I attempted to do in the November/December 1999 issue of the *Porch*.

VIEW FROM THE PORCH

In 1969, during my senior year in high school, I found myself under the tutelage of Mrs. Savage (never knew her first name), one of the best and toughest teachers at South Hall High. I don't know how I ended up in her trigonometry class, but I knew it had something to do with the college prep curriculum I was supposed to be acquiring. It must have worked, because I finally passed college trig on the third try.

Mrs. Savage had divided the class into groups beginning with the brightest, followed by the average, and then us. "Us" consisted of four dumb basketball players and me. Some of these dummies are still alive, so I won't use their last names, but they truly looked dumb with their mouths always hanging open and their long legs and big feet extending out from their desks.

Mrs. Savage had a test prepared for each group, and she usually spent one entire class returning the graded copies and explaining the errors. She always started with the smart kids and then worked her way around to us, the intellectually challenged. As she handed each member of the dummies his test, she would reprimand him by saying, "Oh, David, you so disappointed me. [David had made a 50.] I thought after we worked so hard on this that you were beginning to get it." The only thing David or any of the other players *were* getting was a worried look on their face as they pondered if they would remain eligible for basketball.

And so it went with each dummy, their scores ranging in the 50s—until she got to me. When she handed me my test (a 49), she paused and said, "Homer, you didn't do so well either, but don't feel bad. I've seen your IQ scores." Then her face turned red as she realized what she had inadvertently revealed. It didn't take me long to figure out that I should probably not pursue a career as a nuclear physicist.

Much has been made lately about test scores and other indicators that the public/government school system is failing. The politicians—and especially the teacher unions—insist that more money will solve the problem. They, along with the social engineers, have experimented with trends and gimmicks that now fill the trash bin of public education. "New Math," "phonics," "open classrooms," "outcome-based education," "block scheduling," and, most recently, "no child left behind" continue to suck in money without producing results.

I really wonder if any of these gurus ever stop to talk with the folks in the trenches every day: the classroom teachers. I sure don't claim to have the answers, but being married to a teacher and knowing several others as friends, it is interesting to hear about some of the problems they face daily. Children show up at school these days with a lot more baggage than the pencils and paper in their book packs. They come with emotional and sexual abuse, often accompanied with abandonment and neglect.

One time, my wife discovered, after six months into the school year, that a little girl aged ten had been living in the back of a car with her single parent mom, who worked two jobs. On another occasion, Renee stood helplessly and heartbroken as Family and Children personnel pried a child from her arms to put in foster care because her mother had been sentenced to jail for trafficking drugs.

Could it be, perhaps, that the real battle for our children cannot be won on the campuses of our government schools, but rather in the home? I do know one thing for sure: A lot of us C students would never have made it without one.

Meetings are as much a part of life as disease and pestilence. Regardless of what you do for a living, sooner or later a meeting comes along that you can't get out of. But even if you do, you won't be able to sidestep the one at the PTO, the church, or the neighborhood planning session. My disdain for meetings was the topic of one of the early issues of the *Porch* from April/May 1999.

VIEW FROM THE PORCH

Meetings rank in the same category as root canals with me. Yet from time to time one comes along that is unavoidable. The worst ones for me are in Atlanta, which is about a fifty-minute drive south in some of the worst traffic on the planet except for London or Hong Kong.

The meeting room is usually in some spiffy hotel, where the room temperature is low enough to keep milk from spoiling. One of the oddities in these places is that even with universal no-smoking policies in place, they provide fancy packaged books of matches in the men's room, along with real towels and mouthwash. Although I don't smoke, I do enjoy collecting matchbooks as reminders of all the exotic places I've been, such as Graceland and Holcomb's BBQ in Greensboro, Georgia.

Not too long ago I was notified of the date and time of a mandatory continuing education class that I was cordially invited to attend. A young colleague of mine was "invited" to the same meeting, so we carpooled together, though it was with some reluctance on his part (he unfairly claimed that I had embarrassed him at previous meetings we had attended together). I promised to be on my best behavior and buy him breakfast if he would just drive—a deal that I knew he wouldn't refuse.

On the morning of our departure, we met at one of my favorite breakfast places, Longstreet Cafeteria, which serves the best biscuit and gravy in the South. Dressed in my uniform of the day—khaki britches and a cotton shirt—I somewhat contrasted with my colleague, who wore one of his dark designer suits. I've worked with the boy for some time now, but my attempts to convince him not to take life so seriously have basically been ineffective. While I had a wholesome plate of two eggs over well with sausage, he held his nose and rudely kept looking at his watch while sipping a cup of coffee.

About an hour later, we left our parked car in the $15 per day parking garage and entered the hotel—early, I might add—where my colleague introduced me to one of his peers he had befriended during his first year of training. This man was dressed in the same Wall Street attire as my young partner. As I shook hands with Mr. Wall Street, I detected a smell that reminded me of being gassed during my infantry training at Fort Benning some years ago.

We rode the elevator together to the floor of the meeting room. When the doors opened, I rushed past young Mr. Wall Street to the men's room to wash the tear gas cologne off my right hand. After about five minutes of vigorous scrubbing, I slipped a book of matches into my pocket and proceeded to the meeting.

My colleague had already found a table with just one seat remaining, which he took for himself. So I sat with some strangers, who proved to be friendly when we all introduced ourselves and shook hands. The meeting started, and I reached into my pocket and unwrapped an Atomic Fireball, my candy of choice, to keep me awake until the first break.

As I discreetly started to put the Fireball in my mouth, I almost fainted from a new stench that had found its way onto my hand during the round of handshaking. Apparently, one of the fellows at my table was wearing a cologne or aftershave that was even more offensive than the tear gas. It caused me to drop my Fireball, which rolled under the next table where my colleague sat. I knew then that I had already embarrassed him, less than five minutes into the meeting.

Finally, at the break, the young man to my right asked if I had an extra Fireball to share with him. I had noticed him nodding off a little himself during the meeting, so I generously offered it to him. It was then I noticed that he was the source of the stench that had so shocked my nostrils. I mentioned how much I liked his aftershave and asked him the brand. "Moose in Heat," he replied, and then proceeded to tell me where I could purchase it and the price. I was appalled to hear that the stuff cost more per ounce than uranium!

I left a few minutes before the lunch break and again went to the men's room to wash my hands. But first, I checked the stalls just to make sure that there were no male moose around. After a succulent lunch of Styrofoam chicken, which is always served at these meetings, I sat back down with my young friend and shared my Fireballs with him until we ran out, which was just before the afternoon break.

By this time, I had been able to convince my partner to leave early by offering to buy us each a milkshake at Chick-fil-A. Plus, I told him, we would beat the 4:00 PM traffic. As we made our way to the parking garage, he murmured something about never riding with me again. He did, however, take me up on the milkshake offer.

On the way home, I reflected on how our culture seems to distort what it really means to be a man. This was true when I was young, and it remains true today. The marketers just reinvent the choice of smelly tonics and dress codes. If only we could figure out the truth that real men smell like burped-up baby formula and fresh-cut grass, and that they usually have some playground dirt on their shoes or smudges from small handprints on their car window.

In the early '90s, our church leadership began a concerted effort to encourage church members to go on short-term (usually two-week) foreign mission trips. Personally, I had no desire to go to a third-world country for two weeks. I would have been content to just have my wife write out a check for the cause while I stayed home and prayed for those who went. So when I was approached to go to Panama in 1991, I knew that Panama City, Florida, was not what they had in mind.

The trip to the Central American country centered on helping some long-term missionaries with construction projects that specifically called for a brick mason. Previously, I had bragged about having worked for a brick mason during summer breaks when I was in high school and college, and I had also claimed to have skill in laying brick. In actuality, I was more of a common laborer than a skilled mason.

I quickly said no when they approached me, and I kept on saying no even as I agreed to start the necessary immunizations and get my passport renewed. I can't explain why I ultimately agreed to go, but even as I stepped on the airplane, I did so begrudgingly inside while smiling and looking religious on the outside. I was sure, even though I would not have admitted it, that God was proud of me sacrificing "my" time and "my" money. My halo was shinning brighter than ever before because I was really doing God a favor.

It didn't take but twenty-four hours after I arrived to learn the real truth: *I* was going to be the beneficiary of this trip. Although Renee and I had traveled to some foreign destinations as a reward for my life-insurance peddling efforts, we had always been perceived as the "rich Americans," and treated as such. But this time, our host families in Panama poured their hearts out to us with their hospitality, and we quickly formed bonds of friendship that would ultimately make saying good-bye in a few days a most emotional and difficult time.

Most of our group consisted of middle-class Americans, but by the Panamanians' standards we were indeed rich. Yet no mention was made of our affluence, and no one in the community ever asked us for money. We became friends on equal footing as we worked alongside each other in the 99-degree Central American sun, and I lost a real ten pounds that I had needed to do for some time. I also lost my pompous attitude when I learned that my spiritual gift was digging septic tanks and lining them with blocks. (I couldn't resist writing my name in the wet concrete at the bottom of each tank.)

When we left for the airport to return home, several families accompanied us. One of the people in that group was a man I had worked with each day. We had become good friends, and he had insisted on carrying my bag each step of the way. I could speak just enough Spanish to make a fool out of myself, which I did on several occasions, so our conversation was limited as we waited in line to board the plane.

The man was accompanied by his young twin daughters, probably about age ten or twelve. When we ran out of things to talk about, one of his girls playfully removed my glasses from my nearsighted eyes and put them on. She squinted and giggled from the distorted view, and it was obvious that she did not need to have her vision corrected. Then she put them on her sister. I cannot describe the look that came on the young girl's face. It was as if she had never known that what she was looking at every day could be so clear. Her mouth fell open and she began to survey the airport with wonder. About that time, our flight was called. I'm convinced that about the only real ministry I did on that trip was leaving my glasses in Panama.

The trip did cure me from boasting about my bricklaying talent. The truth is that I'm actually a klutz with no hands-on skills at all. It's a genetic disorder that came from my dad. He taught me how to use a chainsaw and to split wood, but the more delicate tasks, like fixing stuff around the house, were never part of his job description. Consequently, my wife never asked me to fix anything around the house, opting instead to call a friend or a repairman. This fact was well documented in the September/October 2007 edition of the *Porch*.

VIEW FROM THE PORCH

Mr. "Fix It" is my name, and repairing household stuff is my game—kinda. I take repairing stuff around the house to the next level. Let me explain by sharing a recent event as an example.

The commode in the hallway bathroom at my brother-in-law's house had been continually running, though ever so slightly, for some time. Being a person of slothful habits and little enterprise, he had left the repair unattended for some time. On a recent visit, as I exited the aforementioned room, I kindly made a comment to him that if he continued to ignore the problem, the city water department would list him as a public nuisance for wasting water.

"I'll get around to it," he murmured, but remained seated. He was supposedly recovering from a recent surgery, an excuse he continues to use to avoid doing anything productive. Well, it was time for Mr. Fix It to come to the rescue.

"Don't worry," I consoled my immobilized brother-in-law. "I'll take a look at it."

"Leave it alone—you'll make it worse," he jokingly screamed as I turned to re-enter the bathroom.

I proceeded to remove the top of the commode and wiggle the hick-a-maggiger in the bottom of the tank, which crumbled in my hand. Obviously, the malfunction was being caused by a worn-out hick-a-maggiger. Once again, with a little know-how on my part, the problem had been diagnosed and was well on its way to being resolved. I gave my brother-in-law the name of a good plumber and quickly left as the unappreciative brute went into one of his uncontrollable rants brought on by his current affliction and general bad humor.

My skills and efficiency in repair work have reached such heights that my wife, Renee, doesn't even bother me with the trivial stuff that tears up around our house. "Go fix something for your brother-in-law," she is fond of saying, which is fine by me, as I've always been better with a chainsaw or sledgehammer than trinkets like carriage bolts and hex nuts. She even has her own small toolbox and, though I love her dearly, the silly woman goes so far as to hide it from me. She bars me from using any of her tools, especially super glue, which was the result of a small mishap I had with the evil gook and a shoe repair job.

I typically wear a pair of shoes for about twenty years before retiring them (wingtips and loafers are always in style). One time, the sole had come loose from one of my favorite pairs of dress shoes, and the shoe repair shop was going to be closed for the Fourth of July week. I found the super glue under some stuff in Renee's toolbox, which was hidden behind her computer desk. With glue in hand, I proceeded to the privacy of my upstairs office to avoid any interruptions.

Mindful of my last encounter with super glue—which had resulted in my index finger being stuck to my thumb for about a week—I held the shoe sideways and squeezed the irrevocable gunk under the separated sole. I didn't realize that it was coming out the other side until I felt it dripping on the inside of my thigh. Fortunately I was wearing shorts, so there was no damage to a good pair of trousers, although this did change my bathroom habits for about a week.

The main reason I share this experience with *Porch* readers is to tell you what to do when one glues his foot to the floor. Don't panic or call 911; the consequences could be embarrassing. Instead, briskly jerk up, and the carpet will wear off the bottom of your foot in about a week. In the meantime, just call if I can answer any of your home repair questions.

Chapter 4

Raising the Bar of
Cultural Horizons

*Don't be conformed to this culture, but be transformed by
the renewing of your mind.*
—Romans 12:1-2, NASB

MY DAD WAS on the younger end of a litter of nineteen
children. His father's first wife died in the same smallpox
epidemic that also killed his mother's first husband. When they
remarried to form the union that brought Dad into the world,
they each brought a couple of more kids into the merger, before
producing fifteen more.

That would be a big family by today's standards, but it was
not that unusual in the days prior to World War II. Large families
were common in the rural Appalachians. There was no TV, so folks
went to bed when it grew dark, and being north of the slave belt,
a home full of children provided labor on the farm. Eventually,
the last child would leave home, and it would typically not be too
many years later that the aging parents would be moved in with
one of the older children.

When my dad left home during the last year of World War II,
only two sisters remained in the house. By the time I came along
and was old enough to remember my paternal grandfather, he was
living with one of Dad's older half-sisters. Our Sunday afternoon

visits there gave me a peek into Erskine Caldwell's South that he describes in his novels *Tobacco Road* and *God's Little Acre*.

The homes in our community, including the one owned by my maternal grandparents, were usually clapboard farmhouses. For the most part these homes were painted and well kept, though most didn't have the first shred of insulation between the interior walls and the weatherboarding. Many of the trunks of the large shade trees in people's front yards were painted white from the ground up to about head high, and many of the dirt drives were lined on each side with old car tires planted end to end with about half of each remaining aboveground. Yet there were no cars up on blocks or trash strewn about the yards.

Ours was one of the few houses that boasted a lawn. Most of the others in the neighborhood were bare and swept daily. The same was not true of the dilapidated house where my grandfather Myers spent his last years—a fact that my father always regretted.

The scene would have been a great backdrop for a movie about the Depression, with the old house supported by rock pillars that seemed to precariously raise it about three feet off the ground in most places. The space under the floor provided a bedding area for stray dogs that would show up and decide to stay. Yard chickens scavenged the grounds during the day before retiring to the surrounding trees at nightfall to roost. And, for a time, a pig lived under the house.

My dad's sister and brother-in-law, who kept my grandfather, were not necessarily any poorer than most other folks around. It was just that he didn't work and she didn't care, which meant that my grandfather's small Social Security check was their main source of income.

A sympathetic neighbor had given them the pig because he felt sorry for their children (my cousins). They always appeared to be hungry and dirty, because they usually were hungry and always dirty. They gave the piglet a name I can't recall, but I do remember him getting a little bigger on each of our visits. Not realizing the sad dynamics of the situation, I always enjoyed playing with my cousins, crawling under the house, and playing in the falling-down barn and outbuildings around the place.

One time when Dad and I drove into the yard on a Sunday after church, all of the kids were sitting out on the porch with their heads propped on their knees in a general state of grief. On our previous visit, about a week earlier, the pig had reached a weight of about fifty pounds, well below market or slaughter weight. He now regularly wore a bow around his neck and had become a regular playmate of my cousins, following them around the yard as they played games or rambled around the farm. However, it seems that my aunt had developed a hankering for tenderloin, so my uncle had obliged her. None of the kids would eat a bite of their recently deceased friend and companion, and they were in a state of mourning for weeks.

My father never gave any hint that he was ashamed of any of his family, but he worked two jobs while getting a college education to more than provide for me and my sister and live out an example of how to be a husband and a father. One of the many things he did on his meager schoolteacher's pay was take us on vacations, something unheard of in his own childhood. I wrote about one of those many trips in the November/December 2007 edition of the *Porch*.

VIEW FROM THE PORCH

The photograph on the front cover of this issue of the *Porch* includes, along with me, my wife, Renee; our fat pug, Winston; and my father's 1964 Ford pickup. Renee put the Santa Claus cap on Winston so, as she explained later, folks could tell the difference between me and him. The woman can have a mean sense of humor at times.

The truck is a story by itself. My father drove it to work every day for more than twenty years, including the last day of his life. It sat dormant for a couple of years before I started using it again and eventually began the repair and restoration process that continues today.

The memories it carries far exceed the loads of hay, firewood, horse manure, and tons of other stuff that has filled its bed over the years. Many of those memories center around Christmas break, because the truck once carried a camper in its bed and took us on scores of family vacations. During the summertime we went to the Smokies, while during the remaining week of Christmas break we went south to Florida and a national forest campground named Juniper Springs, located in the proximity of where several of the original Tarzan movies were filmed.

The day after Christmas we would start south on U.S. 441 through south Georgia and north Florida, often traveling after dark and taking in all the Christmas lights in the small towns and farmhouses along the route. On arrival, we would spend the next several days in the Ocala National Forest, where I could almost see Johnny Weissmuller swinging from tree to tree to rescue Jane from a horde of threatening baboons or quicksand.

In an attempt to keep my sister and me occupied, and to prevent her from tormenting me on the trip down and back, we were allowed to invite one friend each. One particular Christmas trip, I invited my buddy Sam Davis to be my guest. I can't remember the fellow ogre who joined my sister. As soon as the camper was parked and Sam and I set up our tent (the ogres slept in the camper with my parents), we did what most normal thirteen-year-old boys would do: We went to try to pick up some women.

After successfully sneaking off without the ogres in tow, we headed for the pool, which was actually a 25-foot-deep crystal clear limestone spring that, over thousands of years, had formed a large cavity in the surface of the forest and was now lined with sidewalks. Sam and I had no interest in the geological history of the spring, but we were attracted to it because we knew that a bunch of other teenagers would be there as well. Over half of those teens were girls, and although I don't recall us being very successful with them, we still tried.

Looking back, and knowing what I know now, perhaps the reason for our failure was that most of the thirteen-year-old girls of our day were not interested in talking about football. Perhaps more of an issue was that they were not impressed with the outdated flattop haircuts that Sam and I were still sporting. The Beatles had already made their appearance on Ed Sullivan.

But even a blind pig finds an acorn occasionally. Walking to the snack bar with our bellies drawn in and our chests stuck out, I overheard two olive-skinned, black-haired beauties of about our age conversing in Spanish. As the reflection of the sun off their braces made my eyes squint (making me kinda look like Clint Eastwood), I coolly commented in my best Spanish, "*El cielo es muy azul ahoy*," or something close that translates to "the sky is very blue today." (Please know that one of the few subjects I did better than a C in while establishing my solid 2.0000 in high school and college was Spanish.)

These two lonely exchange students were immediately swept off their feet, which I attributed to my squinted eyes and fluency in their language. They both started giggling and talking faster than I could follow. Still, the conversation went relatively well until one of them turned to Sam and asked if he spoke Spanish. I had two years of Spanish under the late Coach Leonard Walters, one of the best teachers I ever had. Sam, however, had elected French as an easier route to stay eligible for baseball, and about the only French he knew was "Mary Had a Little Lamb," which was sung every day at the start of his class.

I tried to cover for him, explaining that while my friend did not speak Spanish, he did speak French. One of the girls turned to him and immediately switched to speaking in fluent French. Sam

57

stood there for a minute with his mouth hanging open and finally said, "*Oui.*" I was praying that he would not start singing "Mary Had a Little Lamb." By this time our Spanish beauties had begun to take a closer look at our flattops, and they graciously exited our lives forever.

Other than this, it was a great week. Momma would cook every meal while we were camping, but on the way home we always ate out, and Dad would let us order anything we wanted. I don't remember much else about what my parents did on the trip (like most teenage boys, I was self-absorbed), but thinking back, I know that they had chosen to take us along rather than spending the week alone in a hotel with a pool and restaurant. I was oblivious to many of the sacrifices that they made for us at the time. So, even though it's a little late, thanks, Mom, and I trust Dad is listening.

Homer with Buddy Sam at the Pool, "Picking Up Women"

My dad seemed to always be out of step with the current politics. When the "solid South" was solidly Democrat, he voted mostly Republican. But he never referred to himself as a Republican, and I'm certain he never made any financial contribution to the GOP.

I recall him saying something about how we needed to change men's hearts rather than trying to change their minds. I never really took time to understand what he was saying until years later when I attended the first "Promise Keepers" rally held in the Georgia Dome in downtown Atlanta. The best speaker was saved for last. His name was Tony Evans, and he still pastors a large church in Texas today. Tony is a big man, and he is African-American. As he stood before the packed-out football stadium, he had the entire audience of men all laughing—at times with tears in our eyes.

As best as I can recall, here is what he said about politics: "As I look over this audience of over 80,000 men, most of you are white. And most of you white guys vote Republican because you think that the Republican Party will bring this country back to the moral high ground that it should be on."

It got quiet.

He continued, "The rest of you, 20 percent or so, are minorities, mostly black—which is an indictment on us all for not having more Hispanics and Asians here, but that's another discussion. And most of you black guys vote Democrat because you think that the Democratic Party is more sensitive to the social ills afflicting our country."

It got real quiet.

"Well, I've got news for all of you. There is nothing holy about either one." After making this last statement, he held his Bible high in the air and proclaimed, "Only this holds all the solutions."

It was a defining moment for me. Like many young conservatives, I had been hanging my hope on the Republican Party. Suddenly, I began to grasp what my father had said years earlier. Dad watched very little TV. The only programs that he tuned in to watch regularly were *The Red Skelton Show* and Jackie Gleason, and he got his news from Chet Huntley and David Brinkley on the nightly news.

It has to be hard for younger TV watchers to imagine that for several decades of early programming only three big networks provided the news. Although Dad's source of information was limited to the two evening icons on NBC, he still seemed able to read between the lines and think independently—very independently. In the January/February 2009 edition of the *Porch*, I wrote about my father's perspective on TV news and the events that were written between the lines.

VIEW FROM THE PORCH

Like most aging Baby Boomers, my memories of the '50s and '60s include fallout shelters that many of my friends' parents constructed in their backyards and stocked with cans of Vienna sausage and canned peaches in the event of an atomic attack. When I asked my dad why we didn't have one, he calmly answered that when the Russians attacked, we were going camping, because the campgrounds would not be crowded. You would have to have known my father well to appreciate that answer, but that was good enough for me.

In the meantime, government experts, politicians, and especially the news media continued to remind us of the prowess of the Russian Bear and its military might. And, as we learned after the fall of the Iron Curtain, the Kremlin's intentions were real. At the time, a lot of the media and their intellectual friends regularly suggested to us that the Marxist-socialist economic experiment was, and continued to be, a tremendous success.

(By the way, would you *Porch* readers—being some of the most sophisticated in the country—happen to know where Karl Marx died? Answer: not in Moscow or some other bastion of socialism in Eastern Europe, but in London. The intellectual father of equality for all workers never entered a factory in his lifetime, much less worked in one. He never held a steady job. When the money from his friend Engel—which really came from Engel's capitalistic father—stopped, Marx relied on British welfare to support his children, who were taken in by British social workers because they were classified as malnourished. However, the illegitimate son of his mistress was supported for a time by—heaven forbid—a private Christian ministry. Just a little unrevised history. Ah, but I digress.)

The Russian people, by the way, never built many fallout shelters. I know because I got to visit there during the early '90s, right after Ronald Reagan and Margaret Thatcher teamed up to kick down the Iron Curtain. I and some other country bumpkin friends of mine have actually jogged on Red Square.

While I was wandering around the place where thousands of menacing troops and their vehicles had paraded, Bucky Kennedy, a young pastor friend of mine and former college football player, did something that probably no other American who had visited Russia up to that time had ever done. Bucky had got hold of some bad borsch, which had upset his tummy considerably, and he was big-time sick. Still, we had convinced him to take the Red Square stroll with us, as he probably wouldn't be passing through again anytime soon.

As we approached Lenin's tomb, we noticed a young soldier in a bleached-out and unpressed uniform posted at the entrance. It was at that point that Bucky upchucked the borsch and splattered it all over the red brick. By the pale look on the soldier's face, if he had had a bullet in his rifle, I'm sure he would have shot Bucky. But neither he nor Bucky looked as bad as old Vladimir. Apparently, socialism is about as inept at embalming as it is at maintaining a good standard of living.

We also lived for a couple of weeks in the beautiful wooded countryside of Siberia (no kidding; it was August). There were no fallout shelters to be found, but there were plenty of outhouses. It was hard to fathom that the people who almost beat us to the moon had very little in the way of indoor plumbing, and when they did, it didn't work. If you don't believe me, just ask anyone who has been there—except Jimmy Carter.

These outdoor privies were poorly constructed and had neither a light nor a bench. My grandmother maintained an outhouse until

I started the fifth grade, so my visit to a "Roskie," as we fondly called them, was not much of a cultural shock. But try taking care of business in an unfamiliar Siberian outhouse at night without a light or a bench to sit on while holding a book of matches in one hand and a roll of Russian toilet paper, which is very flammable, in the other. You get the idea of the challenges presented. And, by the way, it was my and my companions' observation that socialism does make nearly everybody equal—equally poor and miserable.

So what's the point of all this uncouth outhouse discussion, you ask? First, if you are going to gulag-land, you should take your own toilet paper. Second, although there are exceptions, for the most part you cannot trust the media or their elitist peers in academia. And finally, even though the Egyptians never made it to the moon, they were a lot better at embalming than the Russians.

My middle name is Lockwood, which is what I was called until the sixth grade. When my sister and I changed schools because my father was hired as the new principal, my teacher, Mrs. Sisk, started calling me Homer, my first name. I encouraged this because some of my former classmates had made fun of the name Lockwood, referring to me as "Woodlock," "Keywood," "Woody," and so on. The end result was that about half the folks I know, including most of my family, call me Lockwood, while the other half call me Homer.

As you might have guessed, this has caused some confusion. However, it has also been helpful, like when some "old friend" whom I haven't heard from in twenty-five years, and never really knew anyway, calls me up to tell me about a wonderful new multi-level marketing scheme that is sure to make me rich. I just politely tell these people that it must be my brother they are looking for, and then I give them the other name and a bogus phone number.

But back to Lockwood. The name comes from a war correspondent named Lockwood Doty, who reported from the Pacific theater in World War II. My father, while serving aboard ship, always looked forward to tuning him in when his duties allowed, and he decided to name his firstborn after him. I had always suspected that my dad secretly wanted me to become a writer/reporter, but he would never have imposed a profession on me. He just wanted me to have one.

My dad was a fan of several news commentators over the years and really got into TV news until it became a profession of sensationalism and bias. During the last years of his life, he had basically given up the network news guys and just read more books. My wife pointed out recently how much I am becoming like him, which I took as a compliment, although I think she may have been referring to his inclination toward stubbornness. My sentiment for the news media is very close to my dad's, which I explained in the May/June 2007 of the *Porch.*

VIEW FROM THE PORCH

In one scene in the movie *Men in Black,* covert operative "J," played by Will Smith, is told by his partner that the real news comes from the tabloids. There may be some truth in this.

I've always been intrigued by tabloids, but the only chance I get to view them is when Renee sends me to the grocery store with a shopping list, which isn't very often because I sometimes lose the list and return home with more wholesome staples like Fig Newtons and other essentials such as a month's supply of chocolate-covered raisins. This typically causes her to start murmuring about stuff like milk and eggs, which, in my opinion, are not nearly as essential as Fig Newtons in the event we have a hurricane or tsunami here in north Georgia. Ah, but as Patrick McManus, my favorite writer, would say, I digress.

Back to the tabloids. I'm afraid to pick one up because somebody from our church might see me. It would be better for a good Baptist to be seen with a six-pack of Pabst Blue Ribbon in his buggy than the front cover of a tabloid. Even though I confess my inclination to almost any depravity, I don't watch TV, so it's not the current TV/movie star celebrity that captures my gaze as I patiently wait in the checkout line while the dingbat in front of me searches for her checkbook in the bottom of her cluttered purse.

The last good movie I saw was *Old Yeller,* so I don't know or care to be up on what starlet has lost 80 pounds, or the latest tofu diet, or the latest scoop on who is sleeping with whom. That drivel is just cleverly used, as Will Smith explained, to disguise the real news. That is what intrigues me and causes me to look around for fellow church members before I discreetly slip a copy of the latest tabloid into my buggy.

After all, how can one pass up a headline like, "Missing World War II Bomber Found on the Moon," or "O.J. Confesses to Being the Father of Anna Nicole's Baby"? Or how about, "Chinese Girl Has Bigfoot's Baby," which just confirms my long-held suspicion that the Bigfoot species really exists in remote mountain ranges around the globe and have actually been captured and had weird experiments performed on them by sadistic CIA agents (where is PETA when you need them?).

Truthfully, I've seen glimpses of Bigfeets (my spellchecker is arguing with me again, but it doesn't know the plural of Bigfoot) at twilight on late evenings while fly-fishing a remote stretch of the Chattooga River in the northeast corner of Georgia before it becomes North Carolina. It has happened more than once, and always on those occasions when my fishing partner and quack vet, Ed Quillian, manages to disappear by going to the car and leaving me solitaire in the coming darkness. He excuses this rude behavior as an attempt to get me started home, but the real reason he does it is because he wants to get back to the Chick-fil-A in Clayton, Georgia, before they close. Oops, I digress again.

So what if the real news is, in fact, found in the tabs? And ain't it oftentimes difficult to tell the difference between the stuff we hear and read from AP, *The New York Times, Atlanta Journal,* or CNN and what we read in the grocery store checkout line publications, except that the latter are more fun and creative?

As I pondered this idea of tabloid authenticity, I was inspired to offer you, *Porch* readers, my own version of tabloid reporting. The *Porch* could do locally what the *National Enquirer* does nationally! The first task would be to find some foo—er, some *qualified expert investigative reporter*—who could chase down leads and take the pictures. After considering several local dufuses, I settled on a low-profile and seldom-employed private detective named Virgil Rainwater.

When I finally found Virgil, he was giving blood at the local blood bank. I was impressed with his life-giving generosity until the administering nurse reminded him that this was his third "donation" in the last ninety days and that he couldn't give again until Labor Day. As Virgil collected his $15, he explained that business had been a little slow. He was eager to take on the *Porch* reporting job for lunch each day at Longstreet cafeteria, which I negotiated down to only the days with *T*s. The deal was struck.

Virgil will start investigating the behind-the-scenes unreported stories that will be available only on the *Porch* website—*homersporch. com*. We hope you decide to click in for what is really between the lines and left out of the mainstream media.

On a hot August day sometime in my early thirties, my dad and I finally had a "birds and bees" conversation, except that he did most of the talking. The fact that we had not had this father-son talk before probably had something to do with him knowing that my older peers had already given me a crude version of how bees buzz and birds tweet. Besides, growing up on a farm, I had witnessed the courting habits of creatures from chickens to plow-horses and the resulting activity. More importantly, he had set an example of how a man should live with one woman and how she should be treated.

But on this particular hot summer day, my father started talking about sex. My first thought was to say, "Dad, Renee has brought me a long way in this area, of which your two grandsons are evidence." But I had learned by this time in my life—albeit with some difficulty—that there are times when I should keep my mouth shut and listen, and I suspected that this might be one of those times. Then I began to figure out what he really wanted to tell me, and it wasn't about the mechanics of copulation, be it chickens or humans.

He began by saying that most men who find themselves involved with a woman other than their wife don't wake up some morning at the sound of the alarm clock and think, *Hey, today is a good day to start an affair.* More likely, it begins with a man arriving to the office or workplace where he has been working with a female co-worker for perhaps some time, and though no thought or action by either of them has ever even hinted toward anything inappropriate, on this particular morning he compliments her on her dress, her hair, and so forth. And just maybe he made these comments innocently and without any other intent. But what this man doesn't know is that her husband has not told her that her dress or hair looks good in the past six months or six years, and she is genuinely touched by his compliment.

So, a little later, she brings him a cup of coffee on the way back to her desk, and they talk briefly. The next day, after he brings her a cup, they talk a little longer. And then one day it's convenient for them to walk across the street to the sandwich shop and have lunch together, which all still appears innocent enough. Of course, you know where this is going, and my dad suggested the same, predicting that they would both end up in a hotel or somewhere else in a situation that neither might have thought possible just a few weeks earlier.

I don't know if Dad suspected me of being unfaithful to Renee, because, by the grace of God, I was not. I will always remember the comment of my friend Greg Brezina who, along with his wife, Connie, has been in full-time Christian counseling to couples since his retirement from the NFL. He said to a group of us on the subject of infidelity, "I'm capable of any depravity."

Also, if my dad had suspected me of fooling around, I doubt that he would have approached the issue delicately. From what I'm told, the promiscuity of today's teenagers is a lot more liberal than of my generation. Yet is it not a tragic irony that my generation of the '60s has successfully sold the idea of free love to the successive generations of our children and grandchildren, along with the sexually transmitted diseases, unwanted pregnancies, and heartaches that accompany them?

However, before I start preaching, I must recall what I and any teenage boy would have tried without the constraints of our "Puritan" girlfriends—and the fear of their fathers. This is from the July/August 2004 issue of the *Porch*.

VIEW FROM THE PORCH

Recently, my wife and older sister came across one of my high school yearbooks. When I came into the room I found them kicking and gasping for air, basically in a state of hilarious stupor, as they pointed to a picture of me and my date to the prom. I thought Ruth Ann was beautiful, even though she was flat-chested and stood 6'1" beside me at 5'7".

Our favorite song, which the all-black band played that evening, was "My Girl" by the Temptations. I can only imagine how graceful we looked as we slow danced and the lead vocalist, replicating the voice of David Ruffin, crooned the lyrics. I swirled Ruth Ann about the gym floor in my yellow tux, which complemented the pink dress she wore that resembled Scarlet O'Hara's curtain garment in *Gone With the Wind.*

After some more pointing at pictures and guffaws of laughter at my 148-pound football picture and my other girlfriend, Hilda "Hogette" Honeycutt, I decided it was time to flip over a few pages and point out some of my favorite shots of my sister's high school years. Admittedly, she was a basketball star. One of the action shots showed her distinguishing profile as she forearmed an opposing player. It reminded me that before she had her nose job a few years later, she could have been the mascot for the Atlanta Hawks.

In another yearbook conveniently lying close by, my wife was holding hands with "Mr. Bobcat" (the school mascot), as the charming couple stood for their prom photo. His lizard-scale tux and black loafers with white socks nicely complemented her lime green dress and purple eye shadow.

Was life really more innocent then? I wondered. That question could be asked by any generation, but perhaps it was most applicable to mine, the boomers, who have been the target of marketers of Gerber and Hula-Hoops and who have driven the economy with our gotta-have-it-now spending style. Perhaps no generation has been so diverse yet similar, most "loving" and yet most disillusioned, as the faces of Aquarius wrinkle.

When I was in the seventh grade the Beatles invaded America, and on the Monday morning following their Sunday night Ed Sullivan debut, my buddy Tim Lawson arrived at school with his flattop hair combed down toward his eyebrows. When Tim's dad (who never really liked the Beatles) found out, Tim got a crew-cut, which he wore until he went off to college.

Speaking of college, that and the National Guard (or, in some cases, Oxford, England) was where most of us male-person boomers went to protest the Vietnam War. College was also where a lot of girl-person boomers went to spend their daddies' money and major in getting a husband. The generation that proclaimed nonconformity collectively wore long hair and bell bottoms.

The '70s was an ugly decade for us boomers and for politics (Richard Nixon and Jimmy Carter), auto design (Ford Granada and Buick Riviera), and clothes (double-knit suits and wide clown ties). During the '80s, the fumes of burning those double-knit suits destroyed a large part of the ozone layer. Many of us boomers by this time were attempting our second or third try at marriage and making payments on our BMWs.

An article from the *Wall Street Journal* that appeared in the late '90s suggested that many boomers were turning to religion. I don't know how accurate that article was, but it did raise the question of what our legacy might be. Because a lot of our parents' wealth was spent on our immediate gratification, many of them now found themselves working full-time in part-time occupations and scratching their bald heads, wondering if maybe Dr. Spock didn't know what he was talking about.

For those generations following us, they might do well by doing the opposite of what we did. For starters, stay married to the same person. Lovingly discipline your children. Don't buy stuff until you can afford it, and, even when you can, ask yourself if you really need it. And, finally, know that some things really are important, like patriotism, and some are even sacred, like human life and the God who created it.

Peace, man.

In Europe they're called "water closets." In Central and South America they are called "*baños*," which is one of the critical words you need to know if you visit there. Here in the USA we call them bathrooms or, in the case of a public facility, restrooms. I can't remember what the French call them, because I don't plan on returning there, but a good bit of Paris smells like one. Regardless, I promise not to bring up the subject of outhouses again if you will *allow* me to share this one story about them from the March/April 2004 issue of the Porch.

VIEW FROM THE PORCH

January 20, 2004, was a big day for the Myers family: We had our septic tank pumped! This is the kind of event that can be big in Talmo.

"Did you know that Homer and Renee had their septic tank pumped?" First Local may ask.

"No!" Second Local may reply. "I thought he was having his gall bladder removed. Same difference, I guess."

No human eyes had seen our concrete-entombed tank for more than twenty-five years until Mr. David Williams (a man I would highly recommend for such a project) raised the lid and exclaimed, "Well, you must have raised a healthy family here." I will spare the reader the graphic details, but wouldn't it be interesting if septic tanks could talk? Only the family picture album could produce a more chronological account of a family's going and growing, from newlyweds and young families to empty-nesters to old age. Yes, if our ol' tanks could talk, an interview by Larry King might go something like this:

LK: Well, Myers tank, it has been twenty-five years since you were submerged into the soil of the Myers's backyard. What are some of your more vivid recollections?

Tank: I recall Homer putting me on a five-year installment plan with Candler Concrete, but I think he paid only about two-and-a-half years. It's difficult to repossess a septic tank.

LK: From your experience, what can you tell us about each family member?

Tank: Well, Britt, the youngest son, fed me a lot of teacher notes and graded test papers that were sent to his parents. Those were certainly never signed and returned. Ashley, the oldest son, almost blew me out of the county when he got his Christmas chemistry set and flushed a failed experiment down the commode. As for Renee…that woman has used enough blond hair rinse to do the yellow lines from here to Seattle. And Homer—well, let's just say that the boy has enjoyed a good Southern Baptist diet, which consists of eating half your body weight each day.

LK: What can you tell us about the lifestyle of the Myers family?

Tank: Just the normal stuff. Thankfully, there was never any cocaine or marijuana flushed down here. I only saw blood of any significance twice. The first occurred when Homer cut a tree down on himself, and a limb left a wide gap on his scalp. The second occurred when Homer, again, wrecked the motor scooter that his brother-in-law, Ed the urologist, had given to Britt. On both occasions, Homer decided to call Ed to sew him up rather than incurring the expense of the emergency room, which resulted in disfiguring scars. This just proves that you should never call a urologist to sew up your head or your knee.

LK: What can you tell us about the social life and some of the friends who visited the Myers's home?

Tank: A lot. Carl Cohen, Homer's Jewish friend, consumes large quantities of pork BBQ with liberal applications of hot sauce. And Ralph Mills…well, he is a human garbage disposal.

LK: Would you consider these past years of this family to be happy ones?

Tank: As mentioned earlier, this family has been and continues to be well fed. They eat—or rather gorge themselves—at Nanny's house (Homer's mom) at least twice a week. The boys are grown and gone now, which just leaves Homer, Renee, and Clyde, their obese pug who, thank goodness, is trained to "go" outside. For years they have maintained a normal routine of work and school and a couple of vacations each year. Usually things are quiet on Sunday mornings, as they are out at church. I suspect that the church activity, along with earnest and perhaps desperate prayer, has had a lot to do with this family being able to laugh at, get mad at, and forgive each other during my time with them.

Gainesville, Georgia, which is just ten miles north of our community of Talmo, is known as the poultry capital of the world. My office has been in downtown Gainesville for more than thirty-five years. Each day, I drive down Jesse Jewell Parkway to get to work. Mr. Jewell is considered the poultry industry's first and most innovative pioneer, and most of us in the area are proud of him and our chicken heritage. I had the opportunity to use this fact to make a point with some folks at an insurance convention not too long ago.

After we had sat down to dinner and the introductions were made and the usual small talk about where everybody was from had started, someone asked about the hobbies of each person seated at our table. When my turn came, I briefly mentioned that I enjoyed fly-fishing, tennis, and deer hunting when I could keep work from interfering with them. I did not attempt to expound on any of my hobbies but yielded to the next person as I began to ponder which fork to use on my salad. Before anyone else could speak, one of the female guests across the table immediately began to expound on the evils of deer hunting and how crude and barbaric one must be to pursue such a primitive pastime.

The truth was that I had grown too old and lazy to go hunting, and even though I would get out of bed early enough, I would just sit there and drink a cup of coffee before convincing myself that I would go on into work and try it tomorrow. But as the more sophisticated and condescending girl person preached on about the archaic and cruel act of taking a deer, I could not resist the opportunity to point out that the chicken she was eating probably came from our home town.

This caused her to pause long enough for me to ask her if she had ever seen inside a chicken processing plant. By now Renee was discreetly kicking me under the table, but since I had Ms. Enlightened Person's (and everyone's else's) attention, I continued. I explained that early each morning, all the chickens are asked to exit the trucks and form a single line. They are marched into the processing plant and given a straight razor, which they hold with their two wings. Then, when a loud whistle blows, the chickens commit suicide by cutting their own throat.

Someone changed the conversation to the weather, and Ms. Sophisticated Person did not speak to me again, even when I offered to bring her a cup of coffee from the dessert table.

My lack of cultural finesse has been something I have struggled with my entire life, and I'm sure that I have been held back or missed opportunities that I was never aware of missing, like getting invited to hear Al Gore speak or something. The September/October 2008 edition of the *Porch* illustrated my struggle.

VIEW FROM THE PORCH

Today at lunch, one of my more sophisticated friends offered me his copy of *The New York Times* as we left the restaurant. In a gesture to appear more tolerant and more cosmopolitan, I graciously accepted his most recent edition of the *Leftist Elitist Peoples'* paper, tucked it under my arm, and walked back to my office.

Once behind closed doors, I opened it up, and the first article to catch my discerning eye was a piece on men's scarves in the fashion section. At first glance, I considered whether a winter scarf might enhance my wardrobe and give me a suave appearance like the male models pictured in the advertisement. But after taking a closer look, I realized that the scarves the tall, skinny models were wearing came to just above their belts. The same scarf on me would be below my knees, so I decided to stay with the T-shirt under my button downs for the winter months.

A book review on a new release by author Sharon C. next caught my attention. It seems that Sharon was a reformed sex addict, and the *Times* was giving great publicity to her book about recovery. Everybody but Sharon's old boyfriends should have been happy for her, but because I was in the process of trying to sell my first book, I couldn't help but be envious of the publicity the *Times* was providing to her. Maybe I had selected the wrong subject to write a book about. Of course, my version of a sex addiction book would have been boring compared to Sharon's, as I've been addicted to the same woman for more than thirty-seven years with no hope of recovery.

After reading Sharon's article, everything else in the *Times* seemed to be anti-climactic, so I proceeded to carry it to the recycle bin. But to just throw it in the basket with the accumulation of *National Enquirer* papers and other tabloids seemed to be a desecration, so I decided to put it in the wastebasket with the other garbage. Just as I tossed it, a headline from the financial section flipped out, and I read in bold type: "How to Treat a Money Disorder." Now *here* was something I might be able to use (not that I've ever had a money disorder, but I know some folks who have).

According to the sage who wrote the article, a money disorder (MD) is usually diagnosed by a Money Therapist (MT), an emerging new profession that is usually filled by an unsuccessful stockbroker or unemployed community organizer. Here are some of the conditions with which you might be diagnosed if you go see a MT:

- **Over-Spending Syndrome (OSS).** This is definitely a breakthrough discovery for budget and financial counselors who for years have been trying to help folks with bad spending habits. Now they can tell their clients—er, *patients*—that it's not their fault.
- **Under-Spending Syndrome (USS).** A very rare condition, usually found in a person married to someone with OSS.
- **Financial Infidelity Syndrome (FIS).** A classic example of a person suffering from FIS would be one who buys a new fly rod and then hides it from his spouse person.
- **Financial Incest Syndrome (FIcS).** This is a person who uses money to lord over or dominate the lives of potential heirs. A victim of FIcS might be heard saying something like this: "You better not make Momma mad."
- **Financial Enabling Syndrome (FES).** These folks dump money on their kids either because they feel guilty for not spending enough time with them or they are just trying to get them out of their life. In either case, this action by the parent with FES has been identified as a major funding source for body piercings and green and purple hair among teenagers.

Well, as I write this drivel, our country is struggling with a major financial disorder of our own. Although attempting to identify the source of the problem and offer a solution is well over my pay grade, I will give this one comment that even a country bumpkin like me can understand: No one individual, family, business, or government can borrow themselves out of debt.

And, finally, though I'm as guilty as anyone else of wringing my hands over this, it's good to stop and remember who really owns it all. He is not wringing His hands over the current situation, nor did it catch Him by surprise.

Chapter 5

On Sports and Leisure

Why do you get up early and work late, to eat the bread of painful labors? For He gives to those who seek Him, even when we sleep.
—Psalm 127:2, SRHT
(Somewhat Revised Homer Translation)

THERE IS ONE common trait that signifies a true Southerner, and it is not necessarily the way we talk. Granted, our accent usually identifies our origin, but most of us don't look like the dashing Rhett Butler or sound like Ashley Wilkes, and praise God we don't grin all the time and think like Jimmy Carter. But I digress.

I do know that sometimes it can be difficult to understand our lingo. For several years I did business with an insurance company domiciled in Hartford, Connecticut. One of the ladies in the underwriting department with whom I frequently spoke was from Boston. She was usually a big help in solving my problems, and we developed a business friendship even though we never met each other in person. However, on more than one occasion we would adamantly disagree on the underwriting classification of one of my applicants who might have some minor health problem (like being 5'6" and weighing 320 pounds).

During one such discussion, she was not giving any ground on behalf of my client, and the intensity of the conversation was heating up to argument status. At this point, I called time out and requested an interpreter. Although she still refused to give me what I was pleading for, she found enough humor in my request that it kept the bridge of correspondence between us from burning down.

But I digress again. Back to the trait that is most common among most true sons of the South: We all carry pocketknives. We carry them to church, to ballgames, when visiting funeral homes, and to weddings. We carry them everywhere except the airport, which, along with obnoxious airlines, is the primary reason I don't fly anymore unless it is absolutely necessary.

We would never use our pocketknife as a weapon or as a tool of self-defense (we prefer broken beer bottles or straight-back chairs), but we do use them for everything else from peeling a peach for our granddaughter to tightening a screw on the screen door hinge. There are some folks who think it is kind of back-waterish to carry a pocketknife. They believe this until they need to peel a peach for their granddaughter or tighten a loose screw, and then they want to borrow my knife.

One of the few luxuries that Dad allowed himself was collecting pocketknives. He got started in the early '70s and would stop at out-of-the-way hardware stores and outdoor markets on trips through south Georgia and north Florida to and from camping and fishing trips in the Gulf. The trips were usually for us and our friends, but we had to endure the back roads rather than the faster interstates and patiently wait while Dad searched out the small town hardware stores for another knife that he had not found yet.

Most of the knives he collected were made by W.R. Case & Sons Cutlery in Bradford, Pennsylvania, and Case is, nine times out of ten, the knife you will find in the pockets of men and boys of the South. I've always found it ironic that a company way up north has its biggest market in the South, which speaks well for a 100-year-old company that has refused to move its manufacturing offshore.

This preoccupation with pocketknives is hard to explain, but it has probably been passed down from our ancestors, who found the need for a sharp knife in the everyday activities of the rural South. From trimming a mule's hoof or castrating piglets to cutting a plug of tobacco or just whittling, a man was lost without his knife. This was especially true when he just wanted to take part in a slow motion conversation at the country store, sitting on a wooden barrel or leaning back in a straight-back cane-bottomed chair, just talking or listening—but mostly whittling. I wrote about this in the Fall 2000 issue of the *Porch*.

VIEW FROM THE PORCH

Whittling is almost a lost art form. Along with making wooden rabbit boxes or hitching up a mule for plowing, it is passing quickly into an activity that "my grandfather or uncle used to do."

Before I continue, it's important to note that whittling and wood carving are not the same. Wood carving is where you actually make something. A lot of folks who whittle can carve something out of wood, but whittling is an activity you do while carrying on a conversation and simultaneously trading mules, talking politics, or sitting by yourself propped in a straight-back chair, just thinking.

I'm a whittler from way back. I learned it from my dad, uncles, and other male role models who would whittle while trading coon hounds or discussing the local sheriff's race. My best friend in fourth grade, J.W. Whitlow, and I would whittle out wooden swords during recess at Candler Elementary School to use in defending the Alamo or our pirate ship. (By the way, here I must offer a theory: If public schools came back with recess —unstructured play time—kids would be less inclined to shoot their classmates or blow up federal buildings.) Sometimes other buddies would join us in defending the Alamo or taking Iwo Jima. Although disagreements would arise, they could usually be settled without intervention of a teacher. The only bloodshed we would suffer would be from a punched nose or skinned knee.

As I've mentioned, J.W. "couldn't talk plain," as we put it. Today he would be classified as "orally challenged" and would have to miss recess for speech therapy. But I will always remember the way J.W. would holler, "Remember the Alamo!" He was a true patriot.

Whittling required some patience and a sharp pocketknife. If you were lucky, you owned a real Case pocketknife with three blades. One blade was kept sharp enough to shave the hair off your arm and was used for whittling or peeling apples and such. A second blade might be used for cutting off a piece of plug tobacco (if you were old enough to chew, which in some circles started when you were weaned from breast feeding). The third blade was for cutting wire or for opening a bottle of RC Cola.

I feel so strongly that whittling be preserved as a pastime in our fast-paced sophisticated world that I'm compelled to start a new fraternal organization called the Fraternal Order of Whittlers (FOWs). I've asked my lawyer friend, Tom Jarrard, to draw up the bylaws.

The first rule would require that we not engage in any civic or community work project—most folks are already too busy doing stuff in Rotary or PTA anyway. To be a member in good standing, one would be required to spend a minimum of eight hours per month—two hours each week—fishing, hunting, golfing, frog gigging, or doing whatever else his or her choice of pastime or hobby might be. Extra recognition would be given to those members who took along a grandson, granddaughter, or any other young'un who might not have a dad around.

The Whittler of the Year award would be named at the annual banquet, which would be held at any restaurant that would allow wood shavings on the floor and pulled pork BBQ as the only entrée. Although we would never give out any plaque, if all the dues were collected, we might give out a new Case pocketknife to the Whittler of the Year.

Anyone interested in joining FOW should purchase a three-bladed pocketknife, relax, take a deep breath, and show up at our next meeting.

The image that many folks have of southerners is that we are all four-wheel-driving, dipping-or-chewing, college-football-fanatic, hunting-and-fishing fools. This is not entirely accurate. Most of our women don't chew or dip.

I used to hunt a lot, but in recent years I've given up the pursuit of whitetails for fly-fishing, and though I've never really chewed or dipped much, I haven't taken up smoking a pipe to try to appear intellectual or thoughtful while holding a fly rod. I've always wondered what heavyweight philosophical thought an intellectual fly-fisherman is thinking as he peers reflectively over his nose through the pipe tobacco smoke. I've come to the conclusion that he is considering a way to hook a live night crawler on his dry fly without some of his other intellectual fly-fishing buddies catching him doing it.

The last time I went afield with a gun was last September. A young man in our community had asked me to join in their opening day dove shoot. I was appreciative of the invite until he added that they needed somebody to keep the birds flying. If you've never been to a dove shoot, you wouldn't know that "somebody to keep the birds flying" means some dufus like me who shoots a lot of shells, mostly missing the doves, thereby making them fly around the field for everybody else to shoot.

Apparently, word had gotten out about my last dove shoot the previous year, where I had stirred up so many doves that they blocked out the sun. I shot six boxes of shells, knocking down three birds, one of which I only wounded and finally dispatched by strangulation.

Dove shoots are the inaugural event in the South for other hunting seasons. Deer and rabbit season run all fall and into late winter, followed by early spring turkey season. The only turkey I was ever able to call up was my Uncle Gerald, who actually looks like a tom turkey, but I didn't shoot him because my aunt is so fond of him.

As I recall my outdoor memories, the best ones involve people and places rather than the taking of fish or game. The September/October 2005 issue of the *Porch* was a brief collection of some of those memories.

VIEW FROM THE PORCH

Because of my cosmopolitan demeanor and air of sophistication, some of my acquaintances are often surprised to learn that I am an avid outdoorsman. Most of my friends who have accompanied me into the fields and streams can only shake their head in disbelief and stand in silent awe of my many sporting accomplishments.

Take, for example, my neighbor Jimmy McEver. He is a good father, husband, and citizen, but he is also a brutish game hog. Jimmy cannot allow himself to miss one rising quail, while I, on the other hand, will sometimes allow an entire covey to fly off without so much as removing a feather.

I'm equally generous on the dove field, unlike another hunting companion of mine, Ralph Mills, who probably would've spent a life of incarceration without my influence and who will brag of filling his limit of doves by choosing to make only difficult shots. Conversely, I shoot only doves that are about to light on power lines in order to save them from the horrid death of electrocution.

Another inborn gift I'm blessed with is a sense of direction in the wild. On occasion I've spent an entire day and night in solitude, enjoying nature during the fall deer season, only to be accused of being lost by my sissy Uncle Gerald, who rarely ventures from the shadow of his truck. One time when we were about to enter the woods before daylight, Gerald, in an attempt to provide amusement at my expense, tied one end of a large ball of cord to my field jacket and exclaimed loudly in the midst of the other club members in our camp, "When this runs out, you stop."

I apologize for boasting, but some of my hunting and fishing companions, in their human frailty, are just envious of the trophies I've bagged. One example of this jealously goes back to my longtime friend Ralph Mills. During one of our high school days together, we had discovered a huge wharf rat population at the Oakwood city dump. We filled our pockets with all the boxes of .22 shells that we could buy with our meager means and returned to the dump for an afternoon of rat killing.

Ralph, in an attempt at sportsmanship, insisted on using his single shot. I had opted for my faithful Remington semi-automatic, which would prove to be a life saver. As we stood side by side, deciding on which direction to go, a giant rat emerged from under some milk cartons. Ralph fired first, merely wounding the beast by shooting off a specific body part. The enraged killer rat charged with his white fangs glaring in the sun while Ralph nervously fumbled with a cartridge, trying to reload. As the beast lunged, I calmly aimed and fired, and his twenty-five pound hulk fell at our feet.

Several taxidermists refused to undertake the challenge of mounting my trophy, but we finally found one willing to display the beast, with his snarling mouth and glaring eyes, mounted on a trash can lid. Unfortunately, my wife, who has no appreciation for stuffed wildlife, conveniently "lost" my trophy while cleaning out our attic.

Finally, the most severe example of jealously of my outdoor accomplishments lies in the dark corners of the heart of my brother-in-law, Ed Estes. Ed is a lifetime fly-fisherman who regularly turns his nose up at folks like me who fish with corn or worms and regularly fill our creel limits of trout. Ed is a devout disciple of "catch and release," which is really just a way of coming home from fishing without a single trout and using the catch and release bit as an excuse. "How did you do last Saturday?" "Great, caught several over twenty inches, but released them all, of course." Sure.

Because of Ed's relentless pressure and charges that I was embarrassing the family with my continued worm fishing, I agreed to subject myself to a torturous series of casting lessons at his tutelage. Much to his dismay, I quickly mastered the art of fly-casting, and today I often find other fishermen stopping and staring in disbelief whenever I stand in the middle of a stream and display my natural skills with the fly rod.

However, Ed, along with attorney and longtime fly-fisherman Tom Jarrard, decided that I could enhance my quickly acquired casting skills by taking a lesson. At their insistence, a session was scheduled with Lowe Outfitters and Guide Service of Waynesville, North Carolina. Once again, I so impressed guide Roger Lowe that he finally left me standing in the Tuckaseegee River by myself. I even heard him remark to Tom, "There's nothing I can do for him."

He spent the rest of the day with Tom, who, in my humble opinion, needed his help more than me.

My dad never held a real baseball in his hands until he got into the U.S. Navy in 1943. There, he was invited to join his ship's team as they played a team from one of the aircraft carriers. The game was played on the flight deck, and this so impressed my dad that he told this story more than any of his other navy experiences.

Even if there had been a baseball available on the shelves of the country stores in the vicinity of his tenant farming home, he would not have had any money to pay for it. He did not follow sports closely and, to my knowledge, never made it to a single football game during his years at the University of Georgia because he was either working or going to class on Saturdays.

One sport that he did watch when the rare opportunity arose was the game of the week anchored by Peewee Reese and his color man, Dizzy Dean. Both were elected into Baseball's Hall of Fame, but my dad identified with the All-Star Pitcher "Dizzy" because of his rural roots (he was from the Ozark Mountains of Arkansas).

When I was in about the fifth grade and my dad was serving as principal of River Bend Elementary School, Dizzy Dean made a stop in our area to speak at a fundraiser for some boys' and girls' camps sponsored by a local charity. Diz needed a film projector and, when the head of the charity called Dad to borrow one from the school library, he invited him to meet Dizzy.

My dad had the forethought to stop by a local Western Auto (precursor to Walmart) and pick up a couple of baseballs. Ol' Diz signed them both, and Dad awarded me and my sister one each. I had the rare foresight to put mine up, and I actually forgot about it until years later when I handed my baseball card collecting on to my youngest son. My tomboyish sister, however, took hers out and threw it against the barn wall, and then left it there to be run over by the lawn mower.

There was one thing my father left for my blond-haired, blue-eyed rambunctious sister that she maintains a grasp on even today: animals. My dad was an animal rights person before it was cool to be one. He had grown up on a farm and had seen firsthand a mule or horse whipped and driven to the edge of exhaustion or a cow or bull dehorned with a two-by-four. Throughout the era of his childhood, and for centuries prior, animals were primarily seen as a source of food or as tools for domestic labor, but he still held disdain for anyone who was unnecessarily rough with a farm animal or pet. It was his contention that if a man was mean to an animal, you had better not trust him. He agreed with Proverbs 12:10 that the way a man treated his mule or dog was a good indication of how he would treat people if given the opportunity to do so.

My sister has taken that philosophy to almost the extreme of the fanatical animal rights crowd of today. So it was never a surprise to my mother when Dad would allow one of us to bring home a stray cur or homeless kitten, which my sister did on more than one occasion. We would nurse the vagabond pooch or kitty back to health and then give it to one of our friends or whoever we could con into taking it.

When my sister brought home in her book bag the wormy, mange-infested black kitten that she creatively named "Blackie," it was only supposed to be for a few days until we could find a home for him. Blackie lived at our house for another fourteen prosperous years, supplementing his daily cat food portions with most of the field mice and rabbits found in the woods around our house.

In addition to passing on the animal lover gene to me and my sister, Dad passed on something even better: memories. He was just a lot of fun in spite of his working twelve-hour days while going to school on Saturdays and at least two nights per week. He introduced the game of "kick the can" to us and our friends, which was a country version of soccer and baseball played by running around three bases and home plate. We would play it until it got so dark we couldn't see the can or he would have to leave for a night class or his second job.

On Halloween, he would dress up like an old man and tell harmless ghost stories, spellbinding us and our friends as we sat around a campfire in our backyard. We never went any farther than the beaches of Florida or the mountains of North Carolina on our many vacation trips, but we felt like world travelers. As an adult, I can brag that I've been on five of the seven continents, but as great as some of those experiences have been, they don't compare with the memories of trips to Deep Creek campground in the Smokies or Juniper Springs in central Florida.

Regardless, some of my friends perceive that I'm not as cultured as I perhaps should be, and they have taken loving steps to expand my cultural horizons. I wrote about this in the January/February 2006 edition of the *Porch*.

Homer's Mother Standing Beside the '64 Ford Pickup that Carried the Family and Friends to Campgrounds from the North Carolina Mountains to the Florida National Forest and Beaches

VIEW FROM THE PORCH

Our friends David and Lee Glover have tried valiantly to expand my cultural horizons. David, a former baseball catcher for Georgia Tech and now an avid runner, is a man of varied interests. His pursuits and passions range from classical music to NASCAR racing. He has been blessed in his business, and now he uses those resources to support his full-time ministry to special needs children.

But David also considers me a kind of special needs person culturally, and he does things to help, like taking me and Renee to the Atlanta Symphony. I've always had a deep appreciation for music. I can name almost every Motown artist and I've seen, live, The Temptations, The Tams, James Brown, The Drifters, and a number of other Detroit and Carolina Beach music groups. So I looked forward to the symphony date and the broadening of my musical experiences. And broaden me it did!

Several months later, David, in his continuing effort to bring "culture" into my life, took me to my first NASCAR race. For the benefit of some *Porch* readers who have never had the pleasure of going to either the symphony or NASCAR, I thought it might be helpful to list what I learned from both experiences and to offer what I learned to be accepted protocol at either event, which, as you might have already guessed, have some slight differences.

First, never applaud at the symphony until the more experienced patrons do. Otherwise, you might find yourself being the only person applauding during a pause in the music, resulting in 3,000 people staring at you and embarrassing your host. Conversely, you can strip off naked and do a handstand in your NASCAR seat, and no one will probably notice.

At the symphony, it is considered uncouth to unwrap and rattle the cellophane off the Fireball candy that you just found in the pocket of your Sunday going-to-church coat. However, at the race, it's okay to gargle and wash your mouth out with Coors Light or any other beverage of your choice, and the choices of beverage are plentiful.

Never high-five someone or shout "oh, yeah!" at the symphony, regardless of how moved you may be by the music. But don't be alarmed when, while sitting—or, rather, standing—in your NASCAR seat, a fat woman wearing a tank top and sporting a strategically located tattoo of #3 with angel wings kisses you on the mouth when her favorite driver takes the lead.

Don't get the mistaken idea that only the affluent attend the symphony. I saw more private jets parked at the Atlanta International Speedway than you would see at Hartsfield International, though most of them had "Go Dawgs," "Roll Tide," or green and orange gators on the fuselage.

Of course, there are some things that are appropriate for the symphony that you would not want to do at the racetrack. For example, you could wear a button with the slogan "Stop the Torture at GTMO" to the symphony, and though not everyone would agree with you, no one would challenge you. Wear the same button to the race and the fat lady with the #3 tattoo will feed your button to you along with your slaw dog. (Speaking of tattoos, none of the women at the symphony had one, but several of them had short haircuts that resembled a shoe brush. Just an observation about the difference between the two cultures.)

Finally, although I don't recall how the symphony began, I was really impressed with the ceremony that preceded the NASCAR race. Before the utterance of "gentlemen, start your engines," they said a real prayer (I didn't see anyone from the ACLU standing up to object) followed by the National Anthem while a squadron of navy jets screamed over the grandstands. Kind of made cold chills run up one's back. After that, and for the next three hours, I didn't hear anything but the roar of engines, including the fat lady beside me screaming into my ear (we had become friends by now, and I made every effort to read her lips).

I probably won't be returning to either event anytime soon. The fat lady who has reserved seats beside David's asked for my cell number, so I gave her David's. Also, I've been barred from the symphony. I will, however, take this opportunity to thank David for a wonderful time at both events and hereby offer to return the favor by inviting him to our next chicken fight.

There are many areas of life that we are inevitably forced to alter as we age. While physical activity and exercise is not the only one, it certainly ranks near the top. For many years I considered myself a tennis player, and I met with my friend Bill Dupree weekly for the world championship. Bill kept the championship belt most of the time, but I could beat him often enough to keep it interesting.

On one occasion two younger fellows asked if Bill and I wanted to play them a couple of sets, so we went up against them as a doubles team. During one of the longer points, one of our opponents hit a lob over our heads that was easily going to fall in bounds near the back line. I turned and sprinted as fast as could and jumped as high as I could, but I still missed the ball by a few inches. I watched as the yellow tennis ball hit the backcourt and rolled to the fence, and then turned back to Bill, expecting to hear a word of encouragement like "good try" or "you just missed it." Instead, Bill stared at me for a minute and then said, "Did you know that you now have a two-inch vertical jump?"

Later that year, my CPA friend, Frank "Scrooge" Henry, and I were jogging on a popular running route in Gainesville near his office. I have a gift for spotting coins on the sidewalk and will stop to pick up change ranging from pennies to quarters. Seeing a shiny nickel before us, I paused and reached down to claim it and deposit it in the pocket of my designer running shorts that I had made by cutting off the legs of a worn-out pair of khakis.

When I looked back, I saw a young jogging mother with a jogging baby carriage, occupied by a fat baby, who was obviously gaining on us. When I made mention to Frank that we were about to be passed by a jogging mom with a fat baby in a jogging baby carrier, he accelerated our pace and forbad me to pick up any more coins. But our effort proved to be futile. She passed us, smiled, and said, "How ya'll doing?" To make matters worse, one of Frank's clients, who is an amateur photographer, just happened to be driving by and stopped to make a sequence of shots that captured the whole episode for posterity.

I've graciously accepted the aging process along with the increased pharmaceutical bills, and I'm not at all shy about asking for the senior discount at Chick-fil-A. And I discovered some other advantages that come with senior status, even though some of them might be presumed on my part, like being eccentric and stubborn. Perhaps I've always been eccentric and stubborn, but at least I don't have to disguise it any more. The May/June 2009 *Porch* was my platform to announce and claim my "privileges of aging."

VIEW FROM THE PORCH

Upon the abrupt arrival of my fifty-eighth birthday, I felt inspired to make a list of some of the things I'm not going to do anymore, some of the things I'm going to quit worrying about trying to do, and a few of the things I'm going to at least give some more effort to doing. I know you are waiting on the edge of your seat to know what these are, so here goes.

Never again will I wait indefinitely to eat at one of those spiffy restaurants that provide you with one of those hick-a-magiggers that give you an electrical shock when your table is ready. It's been my observation that most of those places are not really that busy anyway. A closer look at the dining area usually reveals a few empty tables, which tells me that they are not paying to keep good help, even though their entrée prices are comparable to a monthly car payment.

Of course, the very courteous maitre d' will always offer to seat you at the bar for the forty-five minutes while you wait. But what she is really saying is, "Why don't you sit your dumb fanny at the bar and get half snookered on our overpriced booze so that you will leave an outrageous tip for the dingbat who will eventually be your waitress and will rush by your table at least once to bring you cold coffee so that maybe you will be sober enough to drive home?" So, as long as there is a Chick-fil-A and a few good BBQ places around, I'm off the spiffy eating-place routine. I realize that this might inhibit my and Renee's social life with some of our friends, but I've already noticed a trend of them inviting Renee on those occasions when they know I'm off fly-fishing—which, by the way, is one of those things that, by the grace of God, I hope to do a little more of.

Another thing I'm going to stop trying to do is keeping down the growth of hair in my nose and ears. It's just an old man thing, and I find the tweezers to be increasingly more painful. Maybe once a month I will endure it just so I won't begin to look like the wolf man. In the meantime, this will probably reduce my being invited to spiffy restaurants.

Now on to some things I'm going to quit worrying about. No longer will I concern myself with winning the Nobel Peace Prize. Before you start laughing, let me draw a comparison between former winner Jimmy Carter and myself. We're both from Georgia. We both graduated from military schools—Jimmy from Annapolis, and me, albeit by the skin of my teeth, from North Georgia College. By now you may be saying that I never served as president, but let me mention that I did have a pen pal in the fifth grade. He lived in Guam, and my correspondence with him did about as much for world peace as Jimmy has done. But, alas, with Al Gore's selection for the Nobel, I've come to grips with the reality that because I will never be president, to get it I would have to invent something big—like the Internet.

Finally, when some issue or crisis comes up, I'm going to start classifying it into two categories: (1) things over which I have no control, and (2) things over which I do have at least some control or influence. I'm learning that the second category is increasingly getting smaller, while the first group is expanding. I recently heard a wise speaker put it this way: "Give your entire attention to what God is doing right now and don't get worked up about what may or may not happen tomorrow. God will help you deal with whatever hard things come up when the time comes." Thus, because I don't have any control over world events, the climate, or a host of other headline stuff, and because no one from the White House is calling to get my opinion on the economy, I'm just going to concentrate on more important stuff like being a world-class grandfather. I've determined that a granddaughter can love even a person with limited intellect and charm.

One of my friends, on the occasion of my and Renee's thirty-eighth wedding anniversary, smugly suggested that perhaps I had over-married. When I asked my friend to explain, she used the analogy of me buying and owning a high-end Mercedes Benz. When I again pressed her to expand, she said, "Well, if you owned a Mercedes, you would be 'over-car-ed'; likewise, you might be a bit over-married." I reminded her that Renee had failed the submissive wife course at our church. Her only comment, as she rolled her eyes, was that she could see why.

Renee even got in on the fun by suggesting that, as I get older, I'm getting more like my dad. She and Dad got along well, both being teachers and kindred spirits, but that did not keep her from noting his eccentric hang-ups and suggesting that I was well on my way toward acquiring some of them. Then she began to point them out.

My dad would not eat at fast food places; neither will I. Like him, I am happy with a pack of peanut butter crackers from the convenience store or, if I want to indulge, a can of can of Vienna sausages, but not a double-fat burger served by an insolent cashier who has never uttered the words "thank you" or "ya'll come back." (Chick-fil-A is the only exception I make, because all their folks use "thank you" like they mean it, and it's a notch or two above fast food anyway.)

Daddy had an aversion for interstate highways; so do I. Besides, you rarely find a real BBQ place near the interstates. If you're in a hurry, just leave a little sooner.

As I've mentioned previously, both Dad and I had an affinity for pocketknives. We buried Daddy with one of his favorite pocketknives in his suit pocket. I know that he did not take it with him where he was going, and neither will I, but if some archeologist should dig us up someday, perhaps it will tell him something good about our culture.

Finally, Dad had a knack for seeing through the façade and pretense of liking something because it was in vogue and everybody else was embracing it. I'm still working on achieving that one, but in the July/August 2009 edition of the *Porch*, I suggested that I'm getting there.

VIEW FROM THE PORCH

In a recent conversation with some of my aging baby boomer peers in our Sunday school class, I attempted to defend my criticism of some of the art that is being marketed in Christian bookstores. I say some, not all, because I do like some of the art I see. But in what I perceived to be a very non-Christian spirit—much like the judges at the Salem witch trials—my peers were quick to point out that my taste in art could best be classified as impressionist country bumpkin or enlightened Neanderthal.

I countered that this was not necessarily so, and then went on to tell them about an experience I had during the five years I spent at North Georgia College acquiring my four-year degree. I had found myself in a music/art appreciation course. I had to fill a gap with an elective, so I opted to broaden my intellectual horizons and take a music/art appreciation course. I assumed that this would be an easy way to earn five credit hours and possibly even an easy B, which were rare for me.

On the first day of class, I immediately began to have second thoughts. I have no musical talent, and my only previous attempt to express any artistic attribute was in the fourth grade when I carved my initials above Montine Crotwell's inside a heart on the side of a beech tree. When Montine, the toughest kid in the school, discovered my subtle attempt to convey my affection for her, she held my arm behind my back and forced me to use the other to scrape off the inscription with my pocketknife. I would end up marrying a woman just as tough—but I digress.

The head of the music department taught the first six weeks of the quarter, and I was sure that if any part of the curriculum were going to give me trouble, it would be this part. Contrary to my fears, however, professor Beethoven and I hit it off great, especially when he learned that both of us were big Motown fans. I loaned him the Temptations greatest hits on 8-track and finished the first half of the course with a B+. Thinking back, I might have got an A if I had not asked him to return my Temptations tape.

After this success, I was confident that I would do well in the second part of the class. But, alas, things were not destined to go as well with Professor Van Gogh. During one of the first lectures, he was showing slides (this was before the days of PowerPoint) of some abstract art that he had photographed over the years while visiting different museums and art shows. One specific slide showed an old metal watering can with a radiator hose attached to the top of it and yellow paint dripping unevenly over the sides.

As Professor Van Gogh breathlessly described the piece as one of his favorites and attempted to help us unwashed see its esthetic value, I thought it would be an opportune time to impress him with my intense interest by asking a question. So, with all of the sincerity I could mask, I asked if it would make any difference in the esthetic value of the work if the radiator hose had been fastened to the bottom of the can rather than to the top. Immediately after shutting my big mouth, which by now I realized I should have never opened, Professor Van Gogh puckered up and showed his disgust for my esthetically challenged taste by suggesting that I return to the business department and pursue a career in pulp wooding. I received a D in the art half of the class, which, with my B+ from the music half, averaged out to a solid C+. This was still slightly above my GPA.

Back to Christian art, I confess that my taste is more toward "The Lord's Supper" printed on a beach towel than the ceiling of some chapel in Europe. But do you really think that the disciples (or any other member of the heavenly host for that matter) really looked the way da Vinci and d'Angelo depicted them on canvas or in stone? Peter had to look like the rough and tough Anthony Quinn who played him in one of the Bible movies. The Jesus that I read about in Scripture does not resemble the wimpy, dreamy hippie of some of Hollywood's efforts over the years. The man who chased a bunch of money-changing cheats from the temple, verbally rebuffed their mover-and-shaker power broker religious legalist buddies, fed several thousand folks with a handful of fish and bread, and teared up when he saw the disadvantaged being taken advantage of was not a wimp. And if He really is who He claims to be, when He comes back, neither CNN or FOX will cover it. They will be on their knees with the rest of us. Then, perhaps, we will see how He really looks.

There is a big-time misconception in parts of our country that the women of the South are either illiterate toothless creatures walking barefoot behind their man or delicate and naïve Southern bells living protected lives behind the white columns of the big house. Anyone who has ever spent much time south of the Mason-Dixon Line will tell you that our women are just as smart, clever, and controlling of the men in their lives as their sisters up north or out west. They are just a little more discreet in the way they do it.

My mother would be the first evidence I would put forward to make my argument. She loved my father dearly, but she was constantly involved in encouraging, motivating, and, sometimes, mischievously manipulating his life until the day he died. Case in point: Halloween night several years back. My dad was serving as the principal of a school at the time, and the children from the school had been forming a steady stream of trick-or-treaters to my parents' front door. (This was in the days before Halloween had become a gaudy adult event and was still fun.)

Toward the end of the evening, as the horde of elementary age goblins and ghosts trailed off to bedtime with too much sugar in their tummies, Momma said to Dad, "I'm going to take a shower and get ready for bed." She could have just as easily said, "I'm going to go fly the space shuttle," because she knew he wasn't paying any attention anyway. She proceeded to go to the bedroom, strip off naked, and replace her clothes with one of his old raincoats. As she sneaked out the back door, she grabbed the paper grocery sack that she had already cut two holes in for her eyes.

Coming around the outside of the house, she slipped the sack over her head and approached the front door. Daddy, thinking it was a late-arriving trick-or-treater, opened the door to find a woman standing there with a sack on her head and an open raincoat. Dad later said that he immediately recognized the prankster and attempted to lock her outside while he called a deputy sheriff friend to the scene. Momma, however, insisted that he didn't have a clue and was so startled that she was worried he might have another heart attack.

There is no way to know for sure who was telling the truth, but the story illustrates that southern women do not need to be liberated any more than they already are. In the September/October 2009 issue of the *Porch*, I attempted to clear up several other areas of miscommunication that confuse folks not from here, while, at the same time, addressing the delicate sensitivity of our ladies.

VIEW FROM THE PORCH

Many newcomers to the South are understandably confused by some of the words and terms we use. This goes beyond the common stuff like "ya'll," which has actually been adopted in some other parts of the country along with cornbread and real BBQ (there is still hope for our country). What I'm speaking of here are some of the more unique words of southern lingo that are not as commonly heard elsewhere.

For starters, consider the noun "hussy," as in, "I can't believe that hussy is running for president." Reply: "Naw, me neither, especially after what that dufus husband of her's got caught doing with that other hussy in the Oval Office." For that matter, take the aforementioned "dufus," which is rarely used anywhere else but here in the South. It's pronounced like the proper name "Rufus," which is also mostly used in this part of the country. (Now, before you Yankees start snickering, remember that we don't have any men named "Sal" or "Carmen.")

Note that a dufus is different from a "redneck," which is usually associated with good ol' boys riding around in pick-up trucks and shooting road signs while drinking Pabst Blue Ribbon. Although the term "redneck" often carries negative connotations, it can also describe those of noble and courageous attributes. For example: "Did you hear what that redneck Ralph did when that war protester showed up for the funeral of the boy killed in Iraq?" Reply: "Yeah, he broke his jaw and beat him over the head with his own sign. Ralph told the judge that his only regret was that he couldn't milk the cow until the swelling went down in his knuckles."

Conversely, a dufus may be a fellow of good character who just does something stupid, as in, "Did you hear what that dufus Ed did? Bought his wife a fly rod for their anniversary!" Note that the term is not limited in its use to just an adjective or noun. For example: "Honey, that sure was dufus of me to buy you that fly rod for our anniversary. I'm really sorry. Can I move out of the garage and back into the house tonight?"

You may even have observed some poor soul commit a dufus act or have dufussed yourself. I'll confess to one such act that shows how a man, even with good intentions, can pull off a dufus stunt. One time, I was grilling some fish on our deck for our friends Linda and Frank Henry and my mother, who had invited herself along with my evil-hearted sister. Renee had joined the chorus of girls in offering unsolicited advice on how to grill fish. My main goal was to serve the fish hot, which is critically important unless you are serving carp, in which case it doesn't matter (carp is best served to people you don't really like or who have been drinking a lot).

Finally, when everyone was seated at the outside table, I began to take the fish off the grill and place it on each person's plate. In my haste, I hadn't noticed the scented candles that Renee had placed around the table to give it a *Southern Living* ambiance and ward off the insects. As I leaned over the table, I felt heat rising from what I first thought was the fish. At first I was pleased that I was serving it piping hot, but then I realized that the true source of the heat was coming from my burning cargo shorts, which had caught on fire from one of the candles. Naturally, I calmly began to swat out my smoldering shorts with the spatula I was holding while jumping around the deck screaming, "My shorts are on fire!"

All four of the sensitive and delicate women instantly burst into laughter, and they continued to relapse into snickers that progressed to uncontrollable hoots throughout the evening. Frank, the only other man present, offered the only assistance when he yelled, "Take your shorts off, dufus!" As I stood there in my boxers, I was relieved to find that the damage was limited to my cargo shorts.

I hope this gives you a clear definition of the word "dufus" and also some insights into the heart of southern women.

Chapter 6

Granddaughters, Yardwork, Haircuts, and Fly-fishing

*But the loving kindness of the Lord is from
everlasting to everlasting on those who fear Him,
and His righteousness to children's children.*
Psalm 103:17

WHEN OUR OLDEST son, Ashley, was born, it changed my father's life. He had already served as school superintendent during the tense years of integration, and now he found himself trying to convince a five-member school board on an annual basis to allocate at least some funds away from high school football stadiums and state of the art fieldhouses in order to reduce elementary classrooms from an average of thirty-plus students down to a much more effective and teachable number of twenty.

The stadiums always won the day, which just proved that whether it is the U.S. Congress, statehouse, or local school board, it is much easier to be a politician and go with the flow, thereby increasing your odds of re-election, than to stick by your convictions and be a statesman or stateswoman. To say that Dad was becoming cynical might be overstating it, but he was at least finding it more difficult to not become disillusioned. His first calling was as a teacher, not as an officeholder. Ashley's arrival started him back in that direction.

By the time Britt, our second son, arrived, Dad was making plans to resign from his school superintendent duties. Although he transitioned to a principal's job rather than to a classroom, it was to a school in one of the poorer corners of the county, which would eventually be renamed in his honor.

Dad grabbed up our young'uns any time we were willing to give them up, which was often because Renee and I were both working long hours and, in my case, too absorbed in my own life and hobbies to appreciate the gift of two sons. Dad, along with my mother, took them to Disney World by the time they were six or seven. Weekend camping trips to the north Georgia mountains or the beaches of Florida were an integral part of their early years with Grandpa. Although Dad did not retire, he became a full-time grandfather disguised as a school principal.

When both of our sons were little guys, one of Dad's favorite stunts was to bring home an all-day sucker—the big, flat round ones that had every color of the rainbow swirled in them—and give it to a toddler who was eager to spread the sticky stuff around his mouth, ears, and hair. I never really understood or appreciated the kind of enthusiastic attention that Dad gave our sons until February 28, 1992, and then I began to get it. This is from the Fall 2006 issue of the *Porch*.

VIEW FROM THE PORCH

The writer of Genesis tells us that when God made the first female, He called her "woman" because He made her from man. Personally, I believe it happened pretty much that way, but I've always suspected that there was—and is—much more to it than that. First of all, even though women are "from us," they have always had an advantage in controlling things, even if it is in subtle ways. Second, we men have never really been successful in figuring out what women are thinking, and they are coy in keeping us off balance.

The most compelling evidence for this theory is submitted in the person of my wife, Renee. She not only confuses and befuddles me, but also many of our friends who can't imagine why she decided to marry me and put up with me for more than thirty-eight years now. My sister would be next on the evidence list of confusing women. She is consistent in revising the events of our childhood to make her appear innocent and delicate. During our growing up days she was about as delicate as a band of Hell's Angels.

The list continues as I recall childhood playmates and high-school girlfriends who kept most of the slower-maturing males of the same age, including me, always guessing. I had one girlfriend in high school who was 6'2" and flat-chested (I'm 5'7"). Although slow dancing for me was an awkward endeavor, we had a flourishing high school romance until she asked me if I liked her prom dress. Attempting to pay her and the dress a compliment, I said it looked a lot like the curtains in our church sanctuary. We didn't see much of each other after the prom.

Another time when my friend Ralph Mills and I were on a double-date outing, we took our dates to the Hiawassee Country Fair to watch the pig races and then later to Dairy Queen, where we sprung for banana splits for us and them. The evening came with significant economic cost to both of us, including the gas (for which Ralph is yet to reimburse me his half). Apparently, the whole event went unappreciated by our female companions, as neither of them would be seen with us again. We even invited them to go frog gigging with us, which was a privilege offered only to some of our closest buddies, but still without success.

The latest edition of perplexing women to enter into my life came in the form of my granddaughter, Ana Elyse. Having attempted to help Renee raise two sons, I readily admit my ignorance when it comes to little girls. I know most grandparents brag about how handsome or beautiful their grandchildren are, but I rest my case by submitting the accompanying picture. She came out of the womb fashion-conscious. While her physical attributes obviously skipped over any genes from me, Ana shares some of my personality traits, which, when teamed up with her physical beauty, could be dangerous for her parents, teachers, and future boyfriends.

Ana from Cover of That Issue

As pretty as Ana is, I admit that I am a little worried, because her beauty will not always ensure future happiness. Sometimes as I watch her playing, I wonder what her future will be like. So, just in case someone saves her a copy of this newsletter, I would like to make the following wish list/prayer for her.

First, I pray that she will be educated in a setting that becomes her and encourages her to always have the open and inquisitive mind that she has now along with the sensitive heart she has for animals and people. Second, I pray that at an early age she will grasp that there is definitely a difference between right and wrong and that absolute truth is a reality. Third, although it's contrary to what today's feminist movement would have her believe, I pray that she will expect a young knight in shining armor to carry her off on a white horse at the right time in her life, and that he will stay with her as a life mate until earthly death separates them. Finally, I pray that someone will give her a copy of Proverbs 31:10-31 and that she will choose to model it as her lifestyle. In the meantime, I pray that she continues to enjoy riding with me on the tractor and catching spring lizards in the creek behind her grandpa's house.

A close friend of mine called recently on behalf of his son. There are not a lot of things that I can not or will not empathize with a man on, but I can especially identify with concern for a son. His son was a recent college graduate (Spring 2009) who found that this history-making economy that we all find ourselves in does not have a lot to offer college graduates, even one with a stellar GPA and a good work ethic.

The future for these folks is probably not as bleak as some old grumpy men like me seem to think, but I think it is a lot tougher for them than it was for me. When I walked out of my graduation ceremony, I walked directly into a new job—one of several choices I had in spite of my low GPA. I put my diploma into my life trivia box in the attic that also held my football/track lettermen's jacket and arrowhead collection and stepped into the future with the naïve confidence that things would always be the same as they had been so far in my short life.

One of the advantages I possessed—though I did not appreciate it or even recognize it at the time—was the confidence my dad had instilled in me. He had done this not through any pep talks or speeches, but just by quietly loving and supporting me on the sidelines while I stumbled along in school and life in general. That support came with a dual attachment of discipline, which was timely applied for good measure.

A classic example occurred during the summer quarter break between my first and second year in college. I had been working as a mason's helper (mud man) for several weeks, and I had neglected to get a haircut since I had left the North Georgia campus, where, even during the '70s, it was standard procedure for all cadets to keep the military classic close-cut haircut. I was enjoying being able to grow my hair out over my ears and looking like some of my friends who had attended non-military, anti-establishment civilian schools.

Apparently, my dad did not share my effort to comply with the culture. One afternoon when I walked in from work, he simply said, without raising his voice, "You need a haircut." Looking back and considering some of the habits I had acquired after joining a fraternity, I suspect that there was more at issue than just the long hair. However, this provided him the opportunity to say, in so many words, "You are old enough to live the way you choose, but if you live, eat, and sleep here and your momma continues to do your laundry, you're going to have a haircut before you go to bed tonight."

I didn't say a word. I just turned, found the nearest phone, and called a friend who was living in an apartment in town to see if I could move in with him. When he told me what my share of the expenses would be, I realized that it was not within my means as a mud man. So I called my grandmother, who rarely said no to me, but I was shocked when she kindly told me that moving in with her was not an option either.

A few minutes before Mr. Leckie's downtown barbershop closed, I made it through his front doors in time to get a haircut. When I got home, my dad said nothing about how good my hair looked or anything else pertaining to my personal choices or preferences. But a valuable lesson had been taught and learned nonetheless.

Since that day, regular haircuts have been a part of my life, though they are now a little harder to get, as I pointed out in the July/August 2008 edition of the *Porch*.

VIEW FROM THE PORCH

As I've exited young adulthood, "maturing" adulthood (as my church calls it), and am now stepping into "senior adult" status (the term our church kindly uses in place "old codgers"), I have discovered that finding an authentic barbershop has become increasingly difficult.

For the past three years, Dana Coleman has been providing my monthly shearing since her marriage to my CPA friend Kent. Kent is the typical boring and bland accountant who would prefer reading the latest revenue ruling on the tax treatment of offshore pig farming than having a normal conversation with another person over a BBQ sandwich and sweet tea. Dana, on the other hand, is a vivacious friendly embodiment of energy that other people love to be around and talk to not only for her Cajun accent but also for her skill in showing genuine interest in you and your family.

As soon as I am seated in Dana's chair, she begins to ask me about Renee, my granddaughter Ana, and our fat worthless pug, Winston. Neither Kent or Dana, who are approaching their early forties, have been married before. Most of us who know Kent can understand why, but how Dana stayed unhitched that long is still a puzzle. If there is a marriage committee in heaven, I can only imagine the celestial committee chair angel returning to the Throne Room with the assignment of reporting on Kent and Dana's union and exclaiming, "You ain't going to believe this one!" But I digress. Back to haircuts.

My first recollection of a haircut was administered by my Granny England. Since I spent most of my daylight hours rambling around the barn and surrounding woods of her farm, it was just a matter of time before she started cutting my hair. The shears were the manual type, very similar to the same ones my Uncle Gene used to shear the tails and manes on the mules. (Come to think of it, no one ever said that they weren't the same shears.) Granny England could not use the "bowl on the head" technique on me as she did on my uncles and cousins because, as she explained, "his head is oblong" (one of my ears was—and still is—lower than the other).

I soon outgrew Granny's shearing and began going with my dad to Mr. Myron Lackey's barbershop on the ground floor of the magnificent Dixie Hunt Hotel in downtown Gainesville, Georgia. It was a wonderful place for a kid from the county to visit, and the first time I climbed up into the huge ornate barber chair was very exciting for me. Mr. Lackey was a real southern gentleman who always had a stick of peppermint candy for special customers like me. If we had to wait our turn, there were great magazines to scan through like *Field & Stream* or *Outdoor Life*.

An older African-American gentleman stayed busy shining the shoes of a steady stream of businessmen who came each morning for a shave with a straight razor. They discussed politics and the weather while waiting on a shave and shoeshine. The shoeshine man made a big impression on me and honored me greatly one day by letting me "help" him. Unlike many of my friends who wanted to grow up and become firemen or cowboys, I decided then and there that I wanted to be a shoeshine man. Somewhere between high school and college the idea got lost, but if I live long enough, I swear I'm I going to try it yet.

Usually, my Dad would get a haircut on the same trip. This would allow me enough time to go next door by myself (a big deal for a six-year-old) to the Dixie Hunt drugstore, saunter up to the soda fountain, and order a six-cent cherry Coke. Mr. Lackey cut the hair on my oblong head until I went off to college.

North Georgia College has a long history of military heritage, but no places to get your hair cut were provided on campus. The local barbers in Dahlonega, who were tight with the military department, were more than willing to provide the services that every cadet had to have almost weekly. My five years at North Georgia College began in 1969 and went until 1974, so incoming freshmen usually had the flowing locks representative of the culture. It was always amusing to watch a new cadet sit in a Dahlonega barbershop for the first time and explain to the barber how he wanted his hair cut. "Long on top and not too short on the sides," the new cadet would request. "Sure, pal," the barbers, who well knew the drill, would reply. Zip-zip, zap-zap, and sixty seconds later the flowing locks lay on the barbershop floor.

My six-year-old granddaughter, Ana, administered my most recent haircut. The occasion was at my mom's house as we celebrated my sister's birthday. Unbeknownst to me, an evil plot had been conjured up by my dark-hearted sister and Renee to get Ana to ask me for something that I would have to say no to. So they suggested that she offer to give Grandpa a haircut in Nanny's downstairs beauty chair. (My mother is a retired beautician.) I tried to convince Ana that my sister needed a haircut more than me, but she insisted that I sit in the chair.

Granddaughters, Yardwork, Haircuts, and Fly-fishing

I knew Ana was serious when the first clump of gray hair fell on my knees. That's when I negotiated with her to trade the scissors for the pink rollers. All the while, my evil sister and Renee were hooting and encouraging her on. The good news is that Dana was able to blend in the gap the following week, and Ana has since moved on to doing nails. Thankfully, I never wear sandals or go barefooted.

Ana Cutting Hair

After my dad died, Momma bought herself a .38-caliber revolver. Bad idea. Although I'm not a card-carrying NRA member, I do believe in our right to bear arms, just in case some slug decides to invade our home to maintain his drug habit. But Momma, or "Nanny" as everyone (including her breakfast club sisters) now call her, has a gun in the event that a posse is formed to go after some bad guy and the county sheriff needs her help.

Not too many years back, she returned home from a trip to town to find some Hispanic guys meddling around the barn. She stopped her car in the middle of the driveway, which was their only route of escape, and inquired about their reason for being on the premises. When one of them smiled and replied, "Speak no English," she promptly raised the Colt and said, "I bet you *%#@* understand this." (Nanny has been known to use words not appropriate for Sunday school on occasion.)

She then ordered the men to raise their hands in the air while she called 911 for backup. The 911 lady assured her that a deputy would be there soon and asked her to put the gun away, at which point Nanny promptly hung up her car phone. The arms of the accused bad guys soon began to tire, but they quickly found the stamina to keep them raised when she cocked the hammer. Nanny again called 911, and this time suggested that she might have to wound one of them if help didn't arrive soon, because their arms were getting tired (plus she had housework to do). Almost immediately a patrol car arrived, much more to the relief of the bad guys than to Nanny.

The young deputy called me later and told me what happened after he arrived on the scene. He surmised that the suspects were indeed up to no good. When they exclaimed, "This crazy woman is going to shoot us," he turned to them and, out of Nanny's hearing, said, "She is crazy, and she will kill you, so you had better get your *&%#@s out of here and don't come back." When Nanny expressed her displeasure of the deputy letting them go, he tried to explain to her that he had no real grounds to arrest them except for trespassing, which probably would not bring the sentence that Nanny was hoping for (like a firing squad).

I could not talk Nanny out of her pistol (she has a legal permit), and some folks would suggest that perhaps I shouldn't, but I did make her promise that she would confine its use to only her home.

Sometime after the barn event, the husband of one of Nanny's friends at church came up her driveway in a new pickup. Nanny turned off the lawn mower (she still cuts her own grass) and offered a friendly greeting, thinking that perhaps he was returning a borrowed dish or bringing by some homemade bread from his wife. Finally, after some small talk, and still not knowing the purpose of his impromptu visit, she said, "Bubba, [the name has been changed to protect the guilty and his wife], I've got to get back to work. Is there anything I can do for you?"

At this juncture, and with a grin on his face, he offered, "Well, I thought you just might like to enjoy some male companionship." Nanny's temper is well-known by her friends and family, and it suddenly came charging out in the form of her chasing her low-rent intended suitor with the rake she was holding back to the cab of his new truck. My wife happened to witness what happened next. Nanny shared some more expletives and then, flailing the sides and hood of his truck with the steel garden rake, said, "Explain this to Ethyl when you get home."

The point of telling you all this about my momma is simply to explain why she has always been a stickler for keeping the yard in top-notch shape, even though it was never really important to Dad or me. (Also, don't pull up in her yard without calling ahead or if you have less-than-noble intentions.) This is from the November/December 2009 issue of the *Porch*.

VIEW FROM THE PORCH

Yardwork has never been one of my callings. If the ground in front of our house has a green covering and is neatly mowed once a month, what does it matter if it's crabgrass, small weeds, kudzu, or a combination of all three? My wife does not share my opinions on lawn care, and long ago she gave up trying to retrain me on enhancing our modest grounds and took over the task herself.

I say "retrain" because I inherited my lack of seeing the importance of a meticulously groomed yard from my dad, who thought that fishing, camping, and a host of other activities had precedence over yardwork. This might have had something to do with him working a full-time job while also teaching school to provide food and shelter for all of us during my growing-up years. In my case, the demands are more akin to fly-fishing or reading a book, but the gene of avoiding yard work was passed on nonetheless.

This was profoundly pointed out to me through the mouth of babes one afternoon several years back. As my wife drove up our driveway, our youngest son broke the rare silence of the back seat inhabitants and said, "Momma, we're not yard people, are we?" Looking back over our almost forty years of marriage, I've begun to see that she not only is more in tune with what a lawn should look like, but she also sees human behavior and people through a different lens then I do. She was born with a gift for being perceptive and listening to hurting children and adults. Having spent fifteen years in an elementary school classroom and fifteen-plus more as an elementary school counselor, her skills have only been enhanced by what time and experience can do.

At first glance, Renee's profession may sound like a warm and fuzzy way to spend your day, but for those of us who have been married to a teacher for any length of time, we know that there is an ugly and painful reality that they have to deal with on almost a daily basis. I'm never surprised when she comes home with a new account of some heartbreaking story that took place that day. A recent example involved the abandonment and resulting emotional trauma to a third-grader who's mother had to return to jail for violating parole (the mother was using drugs). My wife came home that day with swollen eyes and a torn blouse—the little girl had gripped it with all her might as the DEFACS worker pulled her away from Renee's arms.

In such cases of physical or sexual abuse—often inflicted by a male significant other/stepparent whom the mother is dependent on for meager food and shelter—you begin to see that there is a whole other culture that many of us are isolated from by our subdivision covenants and gated communities. Although we can't understand why a mother would remain in a situation where her children are threatened, her only other option might be to live in the back seat of her car (if she has one), or in a one-room "apartment" that is really a run-down motel room, or in a trailer crowded up against other dilapidated trailers in a "mobile home park" that the county inspector never gets around to looking at. Think I'm exaggerating? Give me just one of your afternoons right here in prosperous north Georgia/metro Atlanta and I will ruin your day. You will come away with some images that will burn on your brain. But it will be the smell—or rather the stench—that will hang with you for a while.

Normally I try to make you laugh in these columns, but a recent incident that Renee was involved in has left me with nothing humorous to talk about. The only help I've been able to offer her over these years is to reluctantly listen as she unwinds and accompany her whenever she delivers the food or blankets collected by the faculty and local churches. This time, it was a young teacher who went to the "home" of a little boy whose personal hygiene was causing him to be ostracized by his classmates. The scene she described was sadly similar to what Renee had often encountered: a trailer with cardboard over the windows and loose sheets of tin on the roof to help slow the leaks. The home was provided with water from an outside spigot, and raw sewage was run from a PVC pipe in the bathroom to a gully behind the trailer. (By the way, in case you're wondering who the landlord is who operates this kind of project, it's usually a respected business person who sits beside you at your weekly civic club meeting or church on Sunday morning—and they vote Republican or Democrat.)

The young teacher turned to her father-in-law for help, and he allowed the family to move into an abandoned farmhouse on his place that he was planning to store hay in. Water, power, and a proper county occupancy permit were secured, and the little boy was able to experience a warm bath for the first time in his life.

I have to be careful not to become cynical when I hear stuff like this. Where are the county inspectors, social workers, and others who should be helping? They are probably overloaded with other cases. The solutions are not always simple. My wife will tell you that there are some good judges and social workers who are doing their best to help. The problems seem to be so overwhelming that many of us just want to send a check to cover our "involvement" and retreat to the security of our homes and neighborhoods where, as Patrick Morley describes it, we pursue personal peace and prosperity.

Each year at Christmastime, I watch two different versions of Dickens's *A Christmas Carol*. There are several scenes that stay with me all year, but the one where the Ghost of Christmas Present opens his cloak to show the two emaciated children always makes me want to leave the room. Dickens wrote the classic and timeless story around the holiday celebration of the birth of Jesus Christ, who said, "I was hungry, and you fed me. I was thirsty, and you gave me a drink. I was a stranger, and you invited me into your home. I was naked, and you gave me clothing. I was sick, and you cared for me....When you did [these things] to one of the least of these my brothers and sisters [the disadvantaged], you were doing it to me" (Matt. 25:35-36,40).

One young teacher is to be commended for taking Christ's directive literally, and there is a child in her class who is exceedingly better off for her effort. But, in fact, even though this teacher will never receive anything for her efforts—nor will she seek any recognition for it—in the end, she will be the primary beneficiary.

This past summer, three buddies from my Sunday school class and I managed to talk our wives into advancing our allowances and letting us take a few days off to go fly-fishing on one of the more remote streams in the Smoky Mountains: Hazel Creek. Actually, our wives were glad to be rid of us, and they celebrated our absence with several days of eating out and shopping. Ah, the bliss of the years of a long marriage....

Rufus the Bear

After about a five-mile hike (which seemed more like ten to a bunch of aging adventurer fly-fishermen who had packed too much groceries and equipment), we arrived and set up our tents. We had just enough time left to get in some fishing on that first day. Yet little did we know that our piscatorial pursuits would be delayed by the arrival of an uninvited guest in our camp, who would spend a good part of the remaining afternoon with us.

We named our 200-plus pound four-footed guest Rufus. Black bears are normally shy of humans unless they have been fed human food, which, we found out later, was exactly what the idiots before us had done. Because of this, Rufus had developed a real taste for human food scraps and couldn't understand why we kept throwing rocks at him to hasten his departure. Finally, Lyman, who is a former marine and combat veteran who served in Vietnam, proceeded to spray Rufus in the snout with pepper spray. Although the spray got into our eyes and throats as well, it served to hurt Rufus's feelings, and he finally left for good.

The next two days were filled with good fishing, and we caught many native brook trout. However, one afternoon Jim Wallace and I took some time away from fishing to find one of the family cemeteries that he had read about in a book about the park. In the July/August 2010 issue of the *Porch*, just after the fishing trip, I wrote about our visit to the Higton family cemetery.

VIEW FROM THE PORCH

If this year's summer vacation travel trends are similar to those of the past thirty years, more people will visit the Great Smoky Mountain National Park than any other park in the country. Most will never get far off Highway 441, which bisects the park from east to west and connects the gift shops of Cherokee to the ski slopes, condos, and crowded restaurants of Gatlinburg. They will view the mist-covered peaks from the pull-offs or picnic on concrete tables alongside the Little River before they arrive at one of the park's most popular destinations: Cades Cove. A small percentage of these tourists will venture on to the Appalachian Trail, which crosses the park from southwest to northeast, or perhaps some other segment of one or the other 800 miles of trails within the park's boundaries. An even smaller number of these folk will traverse the trails that parallel the small rivers of Forney, Eagle, and Hazel, which empty into Fontana Lake.

There is a good reason why many of these areas are among the least visited. Just a few years after the land for the park was set aside by federal decree and most of the families living on it were forced to move, the Tennessee Valley Authority constructed the largest dam east of the Rocky Mountains. The clear deep waters of Fontana Lake were sealed off from civilization, and the remote communities living on these watersheds were soon abandoned and forgotten.

One of these communities was the town of Proctor, which boasted a population of more than 1,000 residents during its peak logging operations—an operation that harvested more than 200,000 board feet of virgin timber in its short existence. All that remains today of this town and its former post office, churches, schools, and homes are a clapboard white house with a green metal roof that the park service maintains at the mouth of Hazel Creek. The forest has reclaimed and recovered any remnants of human activity, so to camp and fish there for native brook trout, one must either hike twenty miles from the dam to get to the mouth of the river or pay the local marina $50 for a round-trip ticket and cross the lake on a pontoon boat.

If you take the boat, another five-mile walk is required to take you deeper into the interior of the Smokies and bring you to the Higton family cemetery. The gravestones found there, most of which are made from local rock, are not unlike the markers found in the cemeteries of Cades Cove and Catalooche communities. However, one particular marker is hauntingly unique in two ways: first, because it faces north, unlike all the others that face east; and second, because the only inscription on it reads, "A BLACK MAN."

One can only speculate how an African-American came to live in an area populated primarily by the descendants of Scotch/Irish and a few remaining Cherokee. Perhaps he was the descendant of a freed or escaped slave, or maybe he came with one of the logging or mining companies. What is known from oral and written accounts is that in 1918 an influenza epidemic reached the Hazel Creek Valley that held a deadly grip on the residents living there. This man nursed many of the sick residents back to health, fed them and their livestock, gathered their crops, and cut their firewood. When he eventually fell victim to the deadly plague, the townspeople buried him in the all-white graveyard—facing north.

No one knows why the surviving locals decided to face the grave of this unnamed "Good Samaritan" to the north. The tradition of facing graves east is based on the biblical prophecy that when Jesus Christ returns in His second coming, those folks whose graves face east will witness His arrival from the eastern sky. Perhaps the northerly direction of this Good Samaritan of Hazel Creek suggests that he will be among the heavenly host welcoming the others home.

One of the gifts that my father had, which I didn't seem to inherit, was the ability to control his temper. Thinking back, I don't recall him getting mad even when a newspaper reporter wrote a scathing article about him, criticizing how he had handled the firing of a popular school system coach. Later when that same employee was investigated for embezzlement, the paper never ran a follow-up article. What my father did exhibit was what some would call righteous indignation for any person or organization that took advantage of the defenseless or disadvantaged.

My evil-hearted sister still tells the story of one of my infamous early-in-life temper tantrums. Even though she was not present when the tantrum actually took place, she refuses to let it die and even embellishes on each succeeding telling. The scene of the crime was a sandy parking lot of a country store in low country South Carolina. The assailant was a monkey; the victim was me.

We nearly always stopped at the country store to buy bait and an RC or NEHI cola. My dad and his younger brother, my favorite uncle, could also get the most recent fishing report from the locals who sat outside under gigantic live oaks and discussed every topic from politics to the best way to heal a dog from mange. In the winter months they moved inside and guarded the pot-belly stove as they propped themselves up in their straight-back chairs.

The time of the crime must have been during one of the winter months—most likely December, since we usually visited around Christmas and fished while my momma and my aunt, along with my sister and girl cousins, shopped all the downtown department stores in Columbia. I was in awe of my uncle Robert because he was a war hero, and most of his friends, retired NCOs and state patrolmen, were "real" men who easily impressed nine-year-old boys. I loved my dad, but it was Robert and his friends who grabbed my imagination. It never occurred to me who the true hero was until years later when I figured out that the real reason we went so often to South Carolina when Robert or his wife called wasn't to fish and visit family but so that my dad could help and encourage his younger brother. Robert had begun to try to kill off the memories of Korea by killing the brain cells that harbored them with alcohol.

I had finished off my pack of salted peanuts and washed them down with a foot-tall bottle of NEHI grape soda when Robert brought me a pack of Juicy Fruit gum for dessert. There may have been another motive—he probably knew the conversation and jokes would soon be inappropriate for nine-year-olds—because he also suggested that I go outside and play with the monkey that was chained to stake next to his small house. He also bought me another pack of peanuts to feed to the raccoons who were enclosed in a chicken wire cage about three feet off the ground.

Robert warned me to keep my hands out of the raccoon cage, but he didn't say anything about not feeding the monkey, which I proceeded to do after I fed all the peanuts to the raccoons. Now all I had was the gum. As I handed the monkey one piece of gum at a time, he would promptly unwrap it with his little paw hands and stuff it in his mouth. But instead of chewing it, he would swallow each stick. I was entertained by his antics, but soon I was down to my last stick of gum. Then the clever idea occurred to me to chew the last piece myself and hand it to the monkey. I think he would have been all right with this, but what he apparently took offense to was that I reassembled the foil in the wrapper and handed it to him. He took the empty wrapper and unfolded it without tearing the paper as he had the previous four pieces. I'm sure an amused smile came across my face as he looked at the empty wrapper. What took place next happened so fast that it was over before I realized I had been attacked. The beast jumped up on my leg and from there to my shoulder where the bite he inflicted would leave a scar that I bear to this day. Then the culprit scampered into the refuge of his house. My Dad and uncle Robert came rushing out of the front door of the store when they heard me crying and screaming and throwing oversized South Carolina pine cones through the door of his house. I quickly showed my wound and pleaded for an opportunity of revenge on the monkey by beating his little hairy head with a stick I had found. But my school teacher father had a way of getting to the real facts of the stories of little boys, and once he figured out what really happened, he calmly said that I got what I deserved. The store owner supplied some liquid antiseptic that stained my shoulder reddish orange for a few days and we got the bait and went fishing. There is more than one Proverb for times like these. "He who is slow to anger is greater than the mighty and he who controls his spirit is greater than he who conquers a city," and another one exhorts us to "Look over an offense."

I thought that when I started fly-fishing, the tranquility and solitude associated with the sport would automatically make me a calmer person and more at peace with myself and my fellow man. Just like those pictures of a guy standing in a trout stream smoking a pipe and soaking in his surroundings, I would become a serene and thoughtful guy. Not so. Maybe I should start smoking a pipe. I recently documented this inclination to lose my cool in the summer 2010 edition of the *Porch*.

Granddaughters, Yardwork, Haircuts, and Fly-fishing

Family Outing in the Mountains. (Notice My Sister's Socks.)

VIEW FROM THE PORCH

A recent article in the *Wall Street Journal* proposed a theory on why we experience bad hair days. Since I've maintained the same haircut since 1969, I didn't read it, but I do know when a bad day is about to start. My most recent one began when Renee ordered me to take Winston, our pug, out to tinkle and take care of other business. It was on one of her part-time work days, and she prevailed in convincing me to take him out, even though I was running a little bit late myself.

Pugs have been a curse in our family ever since our boys were small. Some families have the hemophiliac gene; we have pugs. This fourth one came along at about the time Renee and I were experiencing full-blown empty nest status. He is the most stubborn, obstinate, and spoiled pug of any of his predecessors.

On this day, I had taken Winston to his favorite spot, hoping to rush the process. Not to be. As he lit up a cigarette and gazed at the sky, he looked back at me and seemed to be saying, "Aren't the stars lovely this morning?" I threatened to take him back inside—meaning he would have to sit with his legs crossed all day as he watched the animal channel (his favorite) if he didn't hurry up. When we finally returned to the house, he reclined in his favorite chair while I, now behind schedule, rushed off down the driveway.

As I sat through each red light that I probably would have caught green had it not been for the pug business, my thoughts turned to murder—as in strangling Winston. To make matters worse, I had forgotten a file at the office that I needed for a client meeting that morning. The prior day, I had put my pocketknife into my right pocket to remind me not to forget the file. After taking a few phone calls I shouldn't have taken, I had rushed out the door to the parking lot. When I reached into my right pocket for the car keys, there was my pocket knife. *Hmm*, I thought. *What was that to remind me to do?* I pondered this for a minute before jumping behind the steering wheel. *Must be something I have to do later,* I said to myself.

It wasn't until I was halfway to my destination that I remembered I had put the pocketknife there to remind me to not forget the file. Now I was running late and needed to call the customer to tell him that I was going to be a few minutes late, but because I didn't have the file, I didn't have the phone number. So I dialed 411 for information. When the call was picked up, a voice that sounded like some bubblehead chewing gum while filing her nails asked, "City and state, please?"

"Buford, Georgia," I replied.

"Sorry," Ms. Bubblehead replied. "Did you say Beaufort, South Carolina?"

"No," I said as articulately as my country bumpkin accent would allow, "Buford, Georgia."

"Sorry, did you say Bangor, Maine?"

"No!" I said, raising the volume.

Ms. Bubblehead, now apparently enjoying this little game, then asked, "Did you say Beaumont, Texas?"

"NO!" I screamed into my cell phone. "You dumb %*#@&!" It was at this point that I heard the "voice." I don't know if it was God or not, but it clearly said, *Dummy, you realize that you are talking to a computer, don't you?* I turned off the cell phone, thankful that my pastor and the members of my Sunday school class had not heard the last part of my dialogue with Ms. Bubblehead.

I soon arrived at the client's office and rushed inside. There I was met by my client's office manager, the woman who really ran the place. "Homer," she said, "did you not get the message? Bubba had to go see about a truck that turned over and needs to reschedule to next week." She turned to the receptionist, who was sitting at her desk chewing gum and filing her nails. "Did you not call Homer?" she said. The young woman, who I was sure looked just like Ms. Bubblehead, gave a stupid grin and exclaimed, "Oh! I forgot to call."

Later that day, I visited a friend at the local hospital who may have been having a worse day than me. When I left, on impulse I stepped into the chapel on the first floor. It was empty and quiet, and there was a stand with a book for folks to write down their prayer requests. Here are just a few of the prayers I read as I began to turn the pages.

Dear Lord, help me overcome the heartache I am facing.

Dear God, please give my father peace from his suffering and pain. Release him from his withered body and let him have his heavenly body. He is ready to go.

Dear Jesus, watch over my baby. Let him lay in the arms of our family who are already there with you. Let him know the love of us still here and that we all will be with him soon.

Through watery eyes, I scribbled in the margin, "Lord, forgive me for whining and for calling Ms. Bubblehead a bad name."

Epilogue

THE BABY BOOMER generation is supposed to have begun with those of us who were born when our fathers returned home from World War II (some of our dads didn't come home), and it is said to have ended about 1960, depending on which sociologist's definition you choose. However you look at it, my birth date in 1951 puts me right in the middle of the group.

For some time, I thought of my time and place of birth to be unique. During my formative years, I had glimpses of the rural South giving way to the new South. I watched the agriculture-based economy and segregation-based culture die out—rapidly in the first case and slowly in the latter. Then I met and formed a lifetime friendship with Carl Cohen who, although born in the same year as I, spent his childhood on the streets of Brooklyn, New York.

That's when I began to realize that though we grew up in two distinct cultures, our stories were very similar. I was surrounded by family and blessed with great parents; so was Carl. I went to a rural Southern Baptist church every Sunday, whether I wanted to or not; Carl was forced to attend synagogue every Sabbath with his arm behind his back. My dad was a navy veteran of the war in the Pacific; so was Carl's.

It was only when we compared how our dads were inducted into the navy that our stories began to differ. Although Judge Cohen, Carl's dad, and my father both lied about their age to enter the navy (they were seventeen at the time), their paths to the Pacific theater were vastly different. Judge Cohen was absorbed into the thick of things immediately by way of the rush and bustle typical of the Big Apple. Dad's story involved apples too, but the kinds that are picked from trees.

Today in the north Georgia community of Cornelia, there is a golf community named the Orchard. When my dad was a youth it really was an apple orchard, and he worked there in the evenings after finishing his farm chores at home. On the day before he was to leave for the navy, the orchard owner, who liked my dad and appreciated his work ethic, paid him a silver dollar on top of his regular earnings. Dad thanked him, slipped the silver dollar into his overall bib, and returned home to grab up what few belongings he had for the next day's bus journey to Atlanta.

Dad had never traveled outside White or Habersham counties during his seventeen years. His mother, a big mountain woman whom I respectfully called Granny Myers, gave him some brief but final advice: "Dean, when you get in that navy, you be sure not to use them commodes. You'll get sick if you do." Those were her last words to him. Dad had seen commodes in the restrooms of the service stations in the towns of Cornelia and Clarksville, but he had never sat on or stood in front of one.

When Dad arrived at the Atlanta bus station for the second leg of his trip (by rail to Norfolk, Virginia), he decided to find a place to "see a man about dog," which is Southern slang for going to the bathroom. However, there were no outhouses. There weren't even any woods or bushes close by. As he cautiously walked through the door of the bus station men's room, his mother's words of warning were pressing on his mind. But something else was more pressing on his bladder, so he finally stood up on one of the commodes and dropped down his overall bib.

When he did, his silver dollar also dropped to the bottom of the commode. Years later he would say that the bravest thing he ever did during the war was to reach down into the depths of that disease-laden cistern and retrieve his silver coin.

From the day he received his honorable discharge from the navy until his death, my father seemed to be consistently involved as a positive influence in the life of some other person. It was always with their invitation that folks found him and sought out his help and guidance. He never held himself out as a marriage counselor, but I recall on more than one occasion coming in from school or getting up on a Saturday morning to find my dad meeting with a couple in our living room or on the back porch. Otherwise, his involvement in other peoples' lives was usually on a one-on-one basis.

In my more recent *View from the Porch* articles, as I have attempted to paint a picture of Dad not only as I recalled him from my childhood but also as an adult, I've come to appreciate who he really was. From the barefoot child of tenant farmers who had to quit school in the fifth grade to work on the farm to serving as school superintendent of a public school system of 2,200 employees and more than 20,000 students, it is clear to see that while his life was not easy, it was rich and full. As a father to me and my sister, he seemed to embody the folkness of Andy Griffith, the playfulness of Bill Cosby, and the wisdom of Solomon.

In the January/February 2010 issue of the *Porch*, I attempted to write about the day of my father's death. The piece ended up being wordier than previous articles, but it still failed to say how much he is missed and how much his life influenced the lives of other people.

VIEW FROM THE PORCH

My sister and I were not perfect children, and a number of folks reading this would laugh out loud at even the suggestion that we were. But neither of us ever got a speeding ticket during our teenage and young adult years. I know that Dad never got one either, but Nanny (our momma) made up for the ones we all three missed.

For many years it was the practice of the state of Georgia, along with assessing you a healthy fine, to punch a little round hole in your driver's license for each speeding violation you received. Nanny's Georgia driver's license had so many holes in it that all that was left was her birthday, her address, and a few other pertinent numbers.

One particular hole really infuriated her. The local sheriff, who was a good friend of Dad's, had administered that one. As he stood by her driver's side window and wrote out the ticket, he punched the hole in her photograph right between her eyes. Then he scolded her with the parting remark, "If you weren't Dean Myers's wife, I'd take you to jail."

Daddy died on February 9, 1987. He had signed the paperwork with the Georgia teacher retirement folks and was to officially leave public education in June of that year. Looking back, I'm convinced that the anxiety of anticipating what he was going to do with the rest of his life, along with the effects of smoking cigarettes since his World War II navy days, combined to finish off his heart, which had already suffered an attack ten years earlier.

I was sitting in the examining chair of Dr. Ed Shannon, Sr., who was a local legend himself, when I received the news. Dr. Shannon's patients didn't need any dilation to make their eyes water, because the jokes and humor he supplied along with the eye exam kept their eyes full of tears. In the middle of one of his tales, his nurse stuck her head in the examining room door and said, "Dr. Shannon, you have an urgent call." Not having even a hint that the call had anything to do with me, I tried to look at my watch to see if I was going to make my next sales appointment.

It's uncanny how some of the life-changing events in our lives come at the most unsuspecting times. I had been trying to convince Daddy to go into the quail grow-out business on our farm in Talmo. My thinking had been that we could mimic the successful chicken growers in our area and supply quail to the south Georgia hunting preserves and the high-end restaurants of New York and San Francisco that usually include the small delicate birds on their menu. I was convinced we would grow wealthy while giving my dad something meaningful to do following his thirty-five years of teaching. Looking back at the idea, I'm ashamed to see my own greedy motives in the business plan and how I misunderstood Dad. He needed something to do, but his emphasis had always been more on helping people than making money.

When Dr. Shannon came back, his whole demeanor had changed. He simply said, "Myers, get yourself over to the hospital right now. Your Daddy is not doing too well." As I went out the door, he added, "Call me and let me know how he's doing."

By the time I entered the waiting room on the cardiac care floor of the Northeast Georgia Medical Center, Momma and Dub Jones were already there. Dub, who was also a career educator, had become good friends with Dad after he had competed against him in what was the first bid for both of them in the campaign for school superintendent. Dub and Dad had been having lunch together at a local restaurant following a principals' meeting when Dad started having severe chest pain. It was Dub who rode with him in the ambulance to the hospital, and he must have been the one who called Momma as well. Even though I don't recall Dub saying much, I will always be grateful to him for what he did for us at that critical time for our family.

Some weeks later, Dub told me that Dad was struggling not only with the idea of retiring but also with the thought of leaving education. He had told Dub that he was seriously thinking about taking a job in a rural northern Georgia mountain school system, where the superintendent had offered him a position as an eighth-grade teacher. I wish he had been able to take that job, and I wish that I could erase the quail idea from my memory.

Dr. Sam Pool has a wing of what is now one of the most modern medical facilities in the country named in his memory. He also has a medical clinic that provides hours of free medical treatment for indigent patients, which was given in honor of the hours and years of service he gave after his retirement. He had been Dad's doc for years, and they knew each other on a first-name basis. We often smiled about the fact that Dr. Pool scolded Dad about smoking. Everyone knew that Dr. Pool himself was enslaved to the same nicotine habit that scores of men and women had picked up during the war years.

Although Dr. Pool didn't know me, he knew Momma by her first name. As he approached her from the intensive care room, he put his arm around her shoulder and said, "Illa, Dean is sick. He is damn bad sick." Momma's tears turned to sobs, but she was still able to sign the form allowing Dr. Pool to administer some last-minute procedures to try to save Dad's diseased heart and life.

A few minutes later, Dr. Pool returned to the waiting room and asked if we wanted to come in and speak to Dad. That's when I knew Daddy was dying. When we entered the room, he was lying on his back with a grin on his face.

It was a grin, not a smile. It was the same grin he wore when he was pulling some surprise, like when he hid the new VW Beetle in the barn and gave my sister the keys in a small package at Christmas. It was the same grin he wore when he left his students wondering where the smoke or bubbles were coming from when he demonstrated an experiment in his eighth-grade chemistry class. And it was the same grin he wore for my benefit now as he took Momma by the hand, looked me in the eyes, and said, "Don't let her drive fast." It was his way of not only saying good-bye but also telling me to try to look after my mother, the woman who had been his life-mate for some forty years.

Daddy never shot a hole-in-one, because he never owned any golf clubs. He never had a trophy deer head or wild trout or bass mounted. He never made a lot of money or accumulated much wealth. He never wrote a book, although he always intended to do so. He gave his life to Momma, my sister, and me. We shared him with the thousands of students who came through his classroom. The funeral director who did Dad's funeral told me later that it was one of the largest-attended funerals he had ever done.

It is a tradition in the South, and perhaps in other parts of the country, for the family to receive friends and condolences the evening before the funeral. Because I'm inclined to make a slobbering fool out of myself at times like these, I prayed that I would be able to maintain my composure. This was not so much to avoid embarrassing my masculinity, but for the sake of family and friends who would be passing through the viewing line, many of whom were hurting almost as much as me.

I had done pretty well, and at least a couple of hundred folks had come by offering hugs and handshakes, when a young boy about eighteen moved in front of me in a wheelchair. I didn't have a clue who he was, but I did notice that his eyes grew watery as he got closer. When he got to me, I reached over to shake his hand, and I will never forget what he said to me: "Your daddy made it his business to help me out one time." Then he lost his voice. I had to excuse myself to the men's room to regroup and get myself somewhat squared away so I could finish out the evening.

As I write this, Christmas Day of 2009 is eighteen days away. As I've mentioned, I always watch two movie versions of Dickens's *A Christmas Carol* every year about this time. Renee usually indulges me by making popcorn and doesn't seem to notice when I get teary eyed in some parts. There are several haunting lines that I find profound, but one that always grabs me comes after Ebenezer Scrooge tries to placate the ghost of Jacob Marley by reminding him that in life he was a good businessman. Marley, with the chains of materialism hanging from his transparent person, exclaims, "Business? Mankind was my business!"

The same can be said of my father. Teacher, bi-vocational pastor, friend, counselor, father and husband. Mankind was indeed his business.

If you would like to be added to the mailing list for *Homer's Porch*, please e-mail your address to homer@homersporch.com

WinePressPublishing
Great Books, Defined.

To order additional copies of this book call:
1-877-421-READ (7323)
or please visit our website at
www.WinePressbooks.com

If you enjoyed this quality custom-published book,
drop by our website for more books and information.

www.winepresspublishing.com
"Your partner in custom publishing."

CPSIA information can be obtained at www.ICGtesting.com
Printed in the USA
239640LV00003B/3/P